SCHIESSVORSCHRIFT

FÜR

DIE INFANTERIE,
1887.

THE MUSKETRY INSTRUCTIONS

FOR THE

GERMAN INFANTRY.

TRANSLATED FOR THE INTELLIGENCE DIVISION, WAR OFFICE,

BY

COLONEL C. W. BOWDLER BELL,

AND PUBLISHED BY PERMISSION OF E. S. MITTLER AND SON,
BERLIN.

The Naval & Military Press Ltd

Published by

The Naval & Military Press Ltd
Unit 5 Riverside, Brambleside
Bellbrook Industrial Estate
Uckfield, East Sussex
TN22 1QQ England

Tel: +44 (0)1825 749494

www.naval-military-press.com
www.nmarchive.com

I APPROVE of the following Musketry Instructions for the Infantry, and authorise the War Ministry to issue any explanatory orders that may be found necessary, and to publish any alterations that may be required, provided that they are not of a fundamental nature.

Berlin, 22nd February, 1887.

(Signed)   WILHELM.

(Countersigned)   BRONSART v. SCHELLENDORFF.

To the War Ministry.

CONTENTS.

APPENDICES.

§ 1. Object and Aim of the Musketry Exercises.

THE musketry exercises are intended to give the infantry such instruction in shooting as they require in order to make effective use of their firearm in battle. Accordingly, these exercises form one of the most important branches of duty, and one that must be cultivated in all its details with the utmost care, and encouraged in such a manner, that the infantry soldier, as early as the end of his first year of service, shall be sufficiently trained to use his rifle in actual warfare. The instruction during the remainder of his period of service will be directed to the perfecting and fixing of that which he has already learnt.

Musketry instruction is subdivided into—

    1. Preparatory exercises.
    2. Target practice.
    3. Field firing.

To which are added—

    4. Instructional firing.
    5. Inspection in musketry.

I. PRINCIPLES OF MUSKETRY.

A. General.

§ 2. Form of Trajectories in General.

1. The path through the air traversed by the bullet (or more exactly by its centre of gravity) is termed the *trajectory*.

2. The form of the trajectory is influenced by the velocity, direction and twist, with which the bullet, driven by the force of the powder gases, leaves the barrel, by the force of gravity, and by the resistance of the air.

3. The force of the powder gases would of itself impart a rectilinear, uniform and continuous forward movement to the bullet, in the direction of the axis of the barrel produced.

4. Through the influence of gravity, however, the bullet drops, *i.e.*, it falls during its flight, and in such a way that the longer the falling motion lasts, the greater is the rapidity with which the bullet drops.

5. The bullet, further, must force before it, and to either

side, the air which it meets in its path. In doing this, owing to the resistance offered by the air, the bullet constantly loses velocity, and constantly requires ever-increasing periods of time for its passage through equal portions of space.

6. From this it results that the trajectory is curved, and more so at the end than at the beginning.

7. Accordingly, in order to hit an object at a given height, such a position must be given to the barrel, that its axis produced forward shall be as much raised above the point aimed at as the bullet drops before reaching it.

FIG. 1.

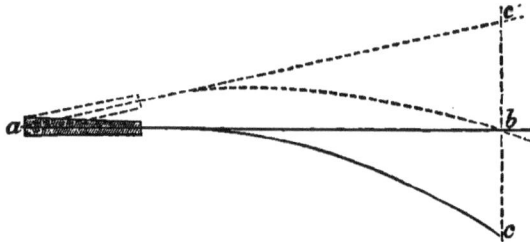

In Fig. 1, *ab* represents the axis of the barrel produced, *b* the object aimed at, *bc* the extent to which the bullet falls in describing the path *ac;* then, in order to hit the point *b*, the axis produced must be raised to the extent of *bc*, that is, it must be directed towards *c'*.

The angle *bac'*, through which the produced axis is raised, is termed the *angle of elevation.*

8. In order that the bullet, which is cylindrical in its longest dimension, shall preserve a constantly definite and regular path, it must always be directed with its pointed end in front. This is attained by giving it an artificial twist about its longer axis, which it retains during its flight; the twist being communicated while in the barrel by means of the grooves.

§ 3. AIMING APPARATUS.

1. The aiming apparatus consists of back-sight and fore-sight. The imaginary line from the middle of the notch of the back-sight to the tip of the fore-sight is termed the *line of sight.*

When this is directed by the eye on a given point, a man is said to aim.

The point on which the line of sight produced is intended to be directed is termed the *point to be aimed at* (*Zielpunkt; Haltepunkt*); the point on which the line of sight is actually directed when the shot is fired, is called the *point actually aimed at* (*Abkommen*); the point in the object where the bullet strikes is the *point of impact.*

According as the point to be aimed at is in the object itself, or at its lower or upper border, we speak of aiming directly at the object, aiming at the bottom of the object (*Ziel aufsitzen*), or at its top (*Ziel verschwinden*).

2. If the line of sight were made to coincide with the axis of the barrel, it would certainly be possible to hit the object by giving greater elevation, but it would often be necessary to select a point of aim above the object, and this would make aiming very difficult and frequently impossible. It must therefore be sought to have the point of aim either on the object or close below it. In order to render hitting possible under this condition, the axis produced must be above the line of sight at the object (Fig. 2), that is, it must cut that line. This is attained by making the notch of the back-sight higher above the axis of the barrel than the tip of the fore-sight is, and further, an arrangement has been adopted by which the elevation of the notch above the axis can be increased as the distance of the object aimed at increases, while the height of the fore-sight remains the same.

FIG. 2.

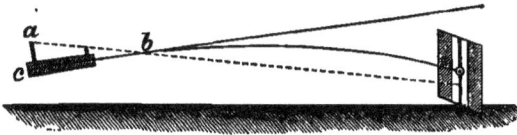

In consequence of this, such a position is given to the barrel, during aiming, that the axis of the barrel prolonged beyond the muzzle is raised as much above the mark aimed at as the bullet falls before arriving at it.

The angle *abc* formed by the inclination of the line of sight to the axis is termed the *angle of sight*.

§ 4. THE SEVERAL PARTS OF THE TRAJECTORY.

The trajectory, *abc* in Fig. 3, at first rises above the line of sight *ac*, in the direction of the axis, and forms the *ascending branch* of the trajectory until it reaches its highest point *b*, the *culminating point*, it then falls and meets the line of sight a

FIG. 3.

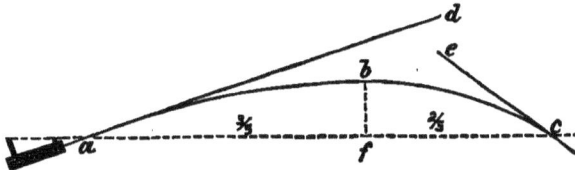

second time at *c*, its course from *b* downwards forming the *descending branch*.

In consequence of the increasing curvature of the trajectory, its culminating point is not in the middle, but somewhere near the end of the third fifth of its course. The ascending branch is therefore longer and flatter than the descending. The former forms with the line of sight the *angle of departure dac*, the latter forms the *angle of descent eca*, which is always the greater.

The perpendicular distance of any point of the trajectory from the line of sight is termed the *height of flight* of the bullet for the particular distance (thus, *bf* is the height of flight for the distance *af*).

The distance *ac* at which the trajectory and line of sight cut each other a second time, and at which therefore the point of aim and point of impact coincide, is termed the *point blank range*, and the shot is said to be *point blank*.

§ 5. EXTRANEOUS INFLUENCES ON SHOOTING.

1. Atmospheric effects.

Wind blowing from a side drives the bullet to one side, and the more so as the distance is greater and the wind stronger. For example, a strong wind blowing at right angles to the direction of fire may produce a lateral deviation of as much as 10 metres (32·8 feet) in 1,000 metres (1093·6 yards). A strong head wind causes a short shot.

The resistance of the air, and consequently the ranges attained, vary with changes in the density of the air (dependent on atmospheric pressure, temperature and humidity). As a rule, ranges are greater in midsummer and less in winter.

Unusually high temperatures have an unfavourable influence on the shooting powers of new rifles.

2. Light.

A fore-sight brightly illuminated from above, appears to the eye, owing to the radiation of the light, larger than it otherwise would; one is apt therefore not to bring the fore-sight sufficiently high in the notch, and so to shoot too short.

On the contrary, dull weather, forest light and twilight, are likely to cause the firer to bring the fore-sight too high in the notch, which results in his shooting too high. If the fore-sight is strongly lighted up from one side, the brightly lighted side appears larger than the darker one; consequently the firer is apt to bring the more brightly lighted part of the fore-sight into the middle of the notch of the back-sight, instead of the tip, and the result is a deviation of the bullet towards the darker side.

B. BALLISTICS.

§ 6. BALLISTIC PROPERTIES IN GENERAL.

1. The ballistic properties, that is, those shooting powers of the firearm which are solely determined in common by the

conformation of the arm and the arrangement of the cartridge, depend upon the conformation of the trajectories, regularity in the departure of the shot (accuracy of fire) and the effect of the bullet.

2. The flatter the trajectories, the more favourable are they.

That portion of ground, measured on the level, within which the trajectory does not pass above the height of the object aimed at (height of a mounted soldier; whole, half, or quarter height of a man on foot), is termed the *dangerous space* (*bestrichene Raum* = "grazed zone"), shown in Plate, Fig. 4. The depth of this space depends in the first place upon the range, and the accompanying constantly increasing curvature of the trajectory, and next upon the height of the objective. At distances under 400 metres (437 yards), the height at which the rifle is held has considerable influence, in so far as the grazed zone increases as the height during aim is lowered; as also, although to a less important extent, the position of the point of aim, since the grazed zone is somewhat smaller when the point of aim is taken at the centre of the object than in aiming low.

3. In consequence of the various circumstances which affect the shooting, bullets fired from the same rifle, and with the barrel in the same position, do not all follow one and the same path; they describe distinct trajectories, which, taken together, are termed the *cone of shots*. This forms a horn-shaped curved cone, the apex of which is at the muzzle (Plate, Fig. 1).

Thus a series of shots, if intercepted by a perpendicular wall, would distribute themselves on a more or less extensive surface of the form of an egg, the vertical axis of which is the greater. This surface is termed the *vertical grouping of the shots* (*vertical shot diagram*). It size increases with the distance of the objective (Plate, Fig. 1).

The centre of such a surface is determined by the position of the central shot, or of a point (O in the Plate, Fig. 2) which has as many hits above as below, and as many on the right as on the left.

The trajectory passing through this central point is termed the *mean trajectory* (o, o^1, o^2, o^3, o^4, b in Plate, Fig. 1).

On the level plane, the shots distribute themselves on an elongated surface, of almost definite length, termed the *horizontal grouping of the shots* or *horizontal shot diagram* (*abcd* in the Plate, Fig. 3), and lie closer together in the middle than at the ends.

The narrower the shot cones and the more compact the vertical shot groupings, the greater is the accuracy of fire.

4. Apart from the resisting power of the objective, the effect of the bullet depends upon its penetrating power and transverse section.

5. The efficiency of powder diminishes the longer it is in store. Stored powder gives diminished ranges, and as a rule less accuracy of fire than fresh ammunition.

6. Taking the rifles together, there are, owing to unavoidable differences in metal, wood, manufacture, &c., some which shoot accurately, others which fire too high or too short. Owing to the effect of the two latter kinds, which exhibit every gradation of variation from the accurately shooting weapons, as well as to the faults of the firers themselves, if a considerable number of rifles be employed at the same time, the cone of shots (Plate, Fig. 5), and consequently the shot groupings, increase in extent, and especially is there a very considerable elongation of the horizontal shot grouping in a rearward and forward direction (Plate, Fig. 5a). In the latter, as the majority of rifles shoot accurately or nearly so, the bullets or hits, as in the case of shots from a single weapon, group themselves most thickly in the middle.

§ 7. BALLISTIC PROPERTIES OF THE RIFLE M/71.84.

1. Velocity of bullet 25 metres (82 feet) from the muzzle, on the average 435 metres (1,427·19 feet).

2. Extreme range about 3,000 metres (3,281 yards), with an elevation of about 35°.

4. *Accuracy.*

Distance in metres	50	100	150	200	250	300	350
„ yards	*54·68*	*109·36*	*164·04*	*218·72*	*273·4*	*328·08*	*382·76*
Vertical dispersion in centimetres	8	16	24	34	44	58	68
Vertical dispersion in feet	*0·262*	*0·525*	*0·787*	*1·115*	*1·443*	*1·902*	*2·23*
Horizontal dispersion in centimetres	8	16	24	32	40	48	58
Horizontal dispersion in feet	*0·262*	*0·525*	*0·787*	*1·05*	*1·312*	*1·574*	*1·902*

Distance in metres	400	450	500	600	800	1,200	1,600
„ yards	*437·45*	*492·13*	*546·81*	*656·17*	*874·9*	*1312·35*	*1749·8*
Vertical dispersion in centimetres	84	98	118	153	280	760	1,872
Vertical dispersion in feet	*2·755*	*3·214*	*3·871*	*5·183*	*9·186*	*24·934*	*61·418*
Horizontal dispersion in centimetres	68	82	96	126	212	460	786
Horizontal dispersion in feet	*2·23*	*2·69*	*3·149*	*4·101*	*6·956*	*15·092*	*25·787*

5. *Penetration.*

1. In wood: the bullet passes through 7·87 inches dry fir at distances under 328 yards, 6·29 inches at 328 yards, and about 2·75 inches at 1,750 yards.

2. In iron: the bullet passes through wrought-iron plates
0·118 inch thick at 656 yards, and causes only bulging in plates
0·275 inch thick.

3. The penetration in freshly thrown up sand is about
6·29 inches at 109 yards, 7·48 inches at 437 yards, 9·44 at
875 yards, 14·17 at 1,093 yards, and 10·63 at 1,312 yards.

Sufficient protection against infantry fire is afforded by
earthen parapets not under about 15·75 inches thick or by
parapets of firmly beaten snow about 78 inches thick. Sheaves
of corn must be at least 78 inches thick to prevent penetration.

II. APPARATUS AND ARRANGEMENTS FOR MUS-KETRY. AMMUNITION.

§ 8. TARGETS.

The frame of all targets is always to be made of wood; the
covering can be made of pasteboard or cloth.

The following descriptions of target are in use :—

1. *Band Target.* (Fig. 4.)

This is 66·93 inches high and 47·24 inches broad. It is

FIG. 4.—Band Target.

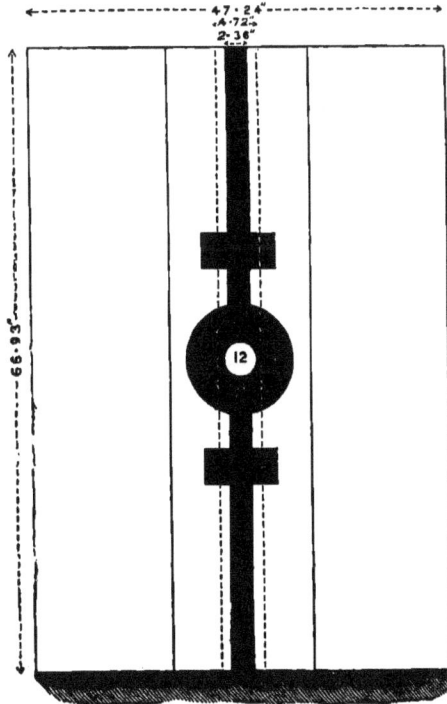

3. *Mean Heights of Trajectory in Metres and Feet**

Sight used.	50 (164)	100 (328)	150 (492)	200 (656)	250 (820)	300 (984)	350 (1148)	400 (1312)	450 (1476)	500 (1640)	550 (1804)	600 (1968)	650 (2132)	700 (2296)	750 (2460)	800 (2…)
Standing sight	0·2 / 0·656	0·3 / 0·984	0·3 / 0·984	0 / 0	−0·5 / −1·640											
Small flap	0·4 / 1·312	0·7 / 2·296	0·9 / 2·952	0·8 / 2·624	0·5 / 1·640	0 / 0	−0·8 / −2·624									
400-metre sight	0·7 / 2·296	1·2 / 3·937	1·6 / 5·249	1·7 / 5·577	1·7 / 5·577	1·4 / 4·593	0·8 / 2·624	0 / 0	−1·2 / −3·937							
450 ,,	0·8 / 2·624	1·5 / 4·921	2 / 6·562	2·3 / 7·546	2·3 / 7·546	2·2 / 7·218	1·7 / 5·577	1·0 / 3·280	0 / 0	−1·4 / −4·593						
500 ,,	0·9 / 2·952	1·8 / 5·905	2·4 / 7·874	2·8 / 9·186	3 / 9·843	3 / 9·843	2·7 / 8·858	2·1 / 6·889	1·3 / 4·265	0 / 0	−1·6 / −5·249					
550 ,,	1·1 / 3·609	2·1 / 6·889	2·8 / 9·186	3·4 / 11·155	3·8 / 12·467	3·9 / 12·795	3·8 / 12·467	3·3 / 10·827	2·6 / 8·530	1·5 / 4·921	0·1 / 0·328	−1·7 / −5·577				
600 ,,	1·3 / 4·265	2·4 / 7·874	3·3 / 10·827	4·0 / 13·124	4·6 / 15·092	4·9 / 16·076	4·9 / 16·076	4·6 / 15·092	4 / 13·124	3·1 / 10·170	1·8 / 5·905	0·2 / 0·656	−1·9 / −6·233			
650 ,,		3 / 9·843		5 / 16·405		6 / 19·685		6 / 19·685		5 / 16·405		2 / 6·562	0 / 0	−2 / −6·562		
700 ,,		3 / 9·843		5 / 16·405		7 / 22·966		7 / 22·966		6 / 19·685		4 / 13·124		0 / 0	−2 / −6·562	
800 ,,		4 / 13·124		7 / 22·966		9 / 29·528		10 / 32·809		10 / 32·809		9 / 29·528		5 / 16·405		3…
900 ,,		5 / 16·405		8 / 26·247		11 / 36·090		13 / 42·652		14 / 45·933		13 / 42·652		11 / 36·090		2…
1000 ,,		5 / 16·405		10 / 32·809		14 / 45·933		17 / 55·775		18 / 59·056		18 / 59·056		17 / 55·775		4…
1100 ,,		6 / 19·685		12 / 39·371		17 / 55·775		20 / 65·618		23 / 75·461		24 / 78·741		23 / 75·461		6…
1200 ,,		7 / 22·966		14 / 45·933		20 / 65·618		24 / 78·741		28 / 91·865		30 / 98·427		30 / 98·427		9…
1300 ,,		8 / 26·247		16 / 52·494		23 / 75·461		28 / 91·865		33 / 108·270		36 / 118·112		37 / 121·393		12…
1400 ,,		9 / 29·528		18 / 59·056		26 / 85·304		33 / 108·270		38 / 124·674		42 / 137·796		45 / 147·640		14…
1500 ,,		11 / 36·090		20 / 65·618		29 / 95·146		37 / 121·393		44 / 144·360		49 / 160·764		53 / 173·888		18…
1600 ,,		12 / 39·371		22 / 72·180		32 / 104·989		41 / 134·517		49 / 160·764		55 / 180·449		59 / 193·573		20…

* The figures in small type show feet; the neare…

NOTE.—These data are founded on a year's shooting with the new powder, M

Distances.

00 324	850 2788	900 2952	950 3116	1000 3280	1050 3444	1100 3608	1150 3772	1200 3936	1250 4100	1330 4264	1350 4428	1400 4592	1450 4756	1500 4920	1550 5084	1600 5248
1 ·281	−3 −9·843															
7 ·966		1 3·281	−3 −9·843													
14 ·933		8 26·247		1 3·281	−4 −13·124											
21 ·899		17 55·775		10 32·809		1 3·281	−4 −13·124									
29 ·146		25 82·022		20 65·618		12 39·371		1 3·281	−5 −16·405							
37 ·893		34 111·550		30 98·427		23 75·461		14 45·933		2 6·562	−6 −19·685					
45 ·640		44 144·360		41 134·517		35 114·831		27 88·584		16 52·494		2 6·562	−6 −19·685			
55 ·449		54 177·169		52 170·607		47 154·202		40 131·236		30 98·427		18 59·056		2 6·562	−7 −22·966	
62 ·416		63 206·697		62 203·416		58 190·292		52 170·607		43 141·079		31 101·708		16 52·494		−2 −6·562

t whole number in the case of distances.

'71, and correspond to the average atmospheric conditions of a year.

painted white and has a vertical black band 2·36 inches broad down the centre.

By means of two vertical red lines, 1·18 inches to the right and left of this band, which are only visible to the marker, an aiming surface 4·72 inches broad is marked off. Hits on this surface are termed "*band hits*."

In the same way two narrow black lines, one on either side of the band, mark off a "*man's breadth*" 15·74 inches wide.

From the centre of the target, with radii of 1·96, 3·93, and 5·9 inches, three circles are traced; these are numbered 10, 11, and 12 respectively, from without inwards, and together form the bullseye.

The red lines which mark off the band 4·72 inches wide are carried across the bullseye. Thus the band is marked on the bullseye, and in similar manner the ring numbered 10 is separated above and below from the black band, and also from ring number 11. 9·84 inches above and below the centre of the target a black oblong patch, 7·87 inches wide and 3·93 inches high, termed the upper and lower "*cross patch*," is marked across the band at right angles to it.

2. *Ring Target.* (Fig. 5.)

This is 66·93 inches high and 47·24 inches broad. 7·87 inches

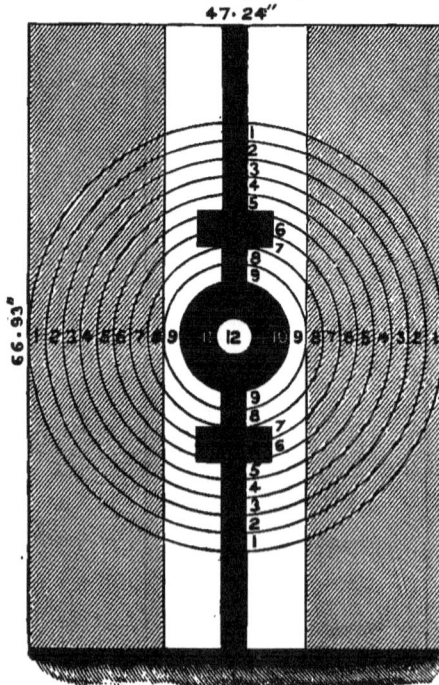

FIG. 5.—Ring Target.

on either side of the vertical central line are drawn the lines marking off the "man's breadth." The latter is white and the two divisions on either side of it, each 15·74 inches broad, are painted a brown colour, resembling as much as possible that of the butt. From the centre of the target 12 circles are described, and the rings so marked off are numbered 1 to 12 from without inwards. The radius of the centre circle, number 12, is 1·96 inches; the radii of the others increase by 1·96 inches each.

The rings 10 and 11 are filled in with black, and together with the 12th form the bullseye.

Down the centre of the "man's breadth" is drawn a black band 2·36 inches wide, which is not carried across the bullseye. The separation of ring 10 from the black band and from ring 11 is shown by red lines.

9·84 inches above and below the centre of the target a black patch, 7·87 inches wide and 3·93 inches high, the upper and lower "cross patch," is marked across the band at right angles to it.

3. *Figure Target and Modifications thereof.* (Fig. 6.)

The figure target is 66·9 inches high, 15·7 inches broad at the widest part, with the figure of an infantry soldier painted on it. Leather belts and trowsers are painted dark.

Fig. 6.—Figure Target.

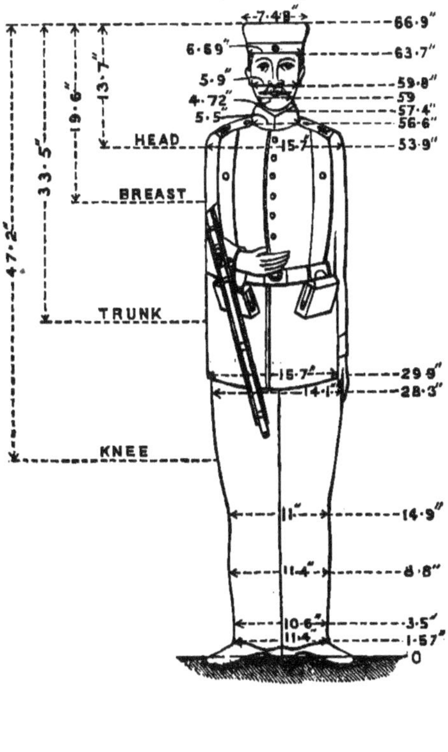

The following modifications are also made by cutting off parts of the figure target:—

    a. Head target, the upper 13·7 inches.
    b. Breast target, the upper 19·6 inches.
    c. Trunk target, the upper 33·5 inches.
    d. Knee target, the upper 47·2 inches.

4. *Section Target.* (Fig. 7.)

This is 66·9 inches high and 78·7 inches broad, and divided into five equal parts (man's breadths) each 15·7 inches wide, of which the centre and the two outer ones are white and the remaining two of a brown colour.

Fig. 7.—Section Target.

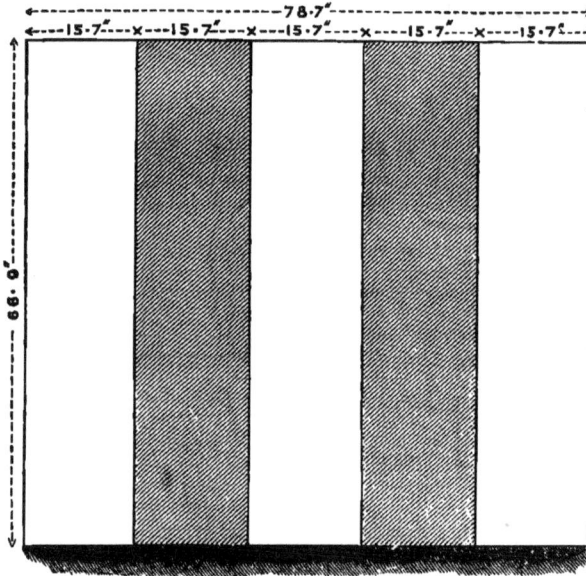

5. Targets which are used to represent objects moving sideways are termed *movable targets*; those which appear for a stated period only, and do not move during such period, are called *disappearing targets.*

The targets may also be constructed so as to move forward or backward, and for this purpose a sledge of corrugated iron is most suitable.

§ 9. SHOOTING APPARATUS.

1. As a preparation for shooting without rest ("free handed") a rest is used (Fig. 8), the notches on which are

marked with numbers, in order that the step on which the
rifle is to rest may be quickly found.

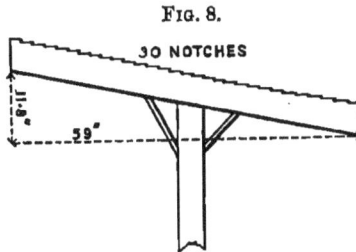

FIG. 8.

30 NOTCHES

2. For target practice (*Schulschiessen*) lying down "with
rest," rifle pits (Fig. 9) or wooden saddles of corresponding
dimensions are to be provided. At ranges with earthworks, the
part on which the firer lies must be raised.

FIG. 9.

Height of Rifle Lying Down + 11·8″

3. Fig. 10 may serve as a type for the construction of parapets and trenches.

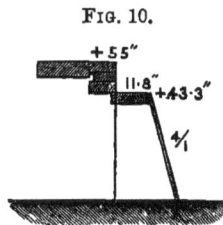

FIG. 10.

+ 55″
11·8″ +43·3″

According to the circumstances of the range, the construction may be more or less sunk in the ground, or not at all.

The firer must be accustomed to making such arrangements
at his post, by removing or adding soil or sods, as shall ensure
him the greatest convenience in firing and loading.

§ 10. FIRING RANGES.

The construction of ranges is regulated by the " Anleitung
für den Bau von Schiessständen."

§ 11. TARGET ALLOWANCE.

Each battalion receives the amount allotted under this head
in the budget.

§ 12. AMMUNITION.

Out of the ammunition allowed to each company there will be put aside as follows :—

1. For field firing 45 rounds per man of the establishment on which the allowance was reckoned ;

2. For the officers' special exercises, 500 rounds ;

3. For the special exercises (§ 14, 3) to be detailed by regimental and battalion commanders, for each non-commissioned officer and man, 10 rounds ;

4. For "instructional firing," 200 rounds.

The rest of the ammunition is to be used for target practice.

No savings are to be made from the rounds put aside for field firing. If such should, however, be unexpectedly made, they are to be used in the field-firing exercises of the next year.

If any rounds are left over from target practice, or from the exercises 2, 3, and 4 above mentioned, they can be used—

(a.) For the further instruction of bad shots.

(b.) For prize-shooting.

(c.) For field-firing exercises.

Special directions as to the employment of the ammunition allotted for musketry inspection exercises are given in Section IX.

Towards the end of the instructional year there may be a surplus of ball and blank cartridge, which, however, will not be very great if the company has been properly managed. This ammunition will be reckoned in the current year as regards giving up empty cartridge cases, &c.; it must not, however, be used up in a reckless and useless manner before the close of the year, but should be utilised at the beginning of the new instructional year for preparatory exercises, or for testing rifles or field firing (compare "Uebungs-Munitions-Vorschrift").

III. INSTRUCTORS.

§ 13. INSTRUCTIONAL PERSONNEL.

1. In the first place the Company Commander is responsible for the musketry training of the officers, non-commissioned officers, and men of the company.

2. The training of the instructional staff must be conducted by the company chief according to the principles laid down in § 15, bearing in mind that the proper education of the men in shooting depends essentially upon the intelligence, shooting ability, and never-flagging energy of the musketry instructor.

3. Officers and non-commissioned officers, therefore, in addition to having a thorough knowledge of the theory of musketry, must acquire such skill in shooting that they shall be able to test rifles and determine any errors in them by means of trial

shots. They must constantly practise aiming and presenting,* in order to retain and improve their skill in shooting.

Every officer and non-commissioned officer must not only be thoroughly instructed in the duties which fall to him in the musketry fight, and be perfectly well able to perform them, but must also be capable of really assisting his company chief in training the men to make effective use of their fire-arms in warfare.

4. To a very great extent the instructor influences the progress of the men in firing by his own personal conduct. He must therefore bear in mind the corporeal and mental peculiarity of the individual firer, and avoid every cause of intimidation. Bad shooting is but seldom the result of faults arising from gross carelessness or laziness on the part of the firer, since the men, as a rule, take a particular liking to this part of their duties, and it is the business of the instructor to preserve and stimulate this feeling.

§ 14. SUPERIOR OFFICERS.

Battalion and regimental commanding officers must systematically and energetically promote the instruction in musketry, while at the same time fully guarding the independence of the company chief. To this end the following means will be adopted :—

1. Aiming and presenting parade by the instructional staff after the commencement of the instructional year, and special examination of the instructors in their duties during the introductory stages of the recruit's instruction in musketry.

2. Inspection of the recruits in aiming.

3. Institution of special exercises in target practice with aiming ammunition and ball cartridge, under the personal direction and supervision of the superior officers (ring target, standing position).

4. Minute inspection of the preparatory instruction for field firing (judging distance, employment of the arm, fire direction, and fire discipline).

5. Holding field-firing exercises for formed bodies and instructional firing exercises.

Particular attention is constantly to be devoted to the personal skill of officers in shooting.

The Commanding Generals, the Divisional and Brigade Commanders, by means of proposing special exercises at the time of their inspections, are enabled to compare the efficiency of the several corps of troops in target practice, and at the same time ascertain whether the instructional staff and men are properly trained in the duties which devolve upon them in firing in the field.

* For the distinction here made see footnote, p. 20.—TRANSLATOR.

IV. COURSE OF INSTRUCTION.

§ 15. MODE OF INSTRUCTION.

1. The instruction of the man must proceed gradually. In all practices the peculiarities of the man must be taken into consideration, and above all things accuracy should be looked for rather than uniformity.

2. The preliminary exercises are begun by the instructor explaining to the recruit in an intelligible manner all that takes place in a rifle when it is fired, then the apparatus for aiming, and the meaning of aiming. At the same time the arrangement of the targets is explained.

In the lessons in aiming which follow next, the man is taught how to grasp the small of the butt, and fire the rifle when fixed on a rest.

Side by side with these exercises such gymnastic exercises, without and with the rifle, are to be practised as are specially calculated to supple the joints which come into play in shooting and to strengthen the muscles of the arm (bending and turning the head, bending and turning the trunk, extension and flexion of the arms, closing the hands, extending the rifle, raising and lowering it, extending it laterally, and waving it round).

Next, the presenting exercises are practised : the placing of the feet (at first without and then with the rifle), coming to the "Ready," * and bringing the rifle to the shoulder in the "Present, standing," with the hands free. Tiring the men is to be avoided; and the men should not be kept too long in the same position.

When the position of the man in presenting,† without support for the hands, is sufficiently good, exercises in aiming without rests will be commenced; and in doing this there will be no attempt, in the first instance, at placing the forefinger correctly round the trigger, or pulling off. Subsequently the operations of presenting, aiming, and pulling off will be combined—at first in the standing position with rest, and afterwards standing free-handed.

After the exercises in presenting free-handed, instruction is given in presenting lying down, kneeling, behind breastworks, in rifle pits, behind the trunk of a tree, against moving objects,

* The motions of the firing exercise are described in detail in the " Exerzir-Reglement für die Infanterie," 1888.

† In the German firing exercise the following distinct acts are performed in the act of firing :—

Anschlagen = coming to the present, of which there are several forms, *e.g.*, standing, kneeling.

Druckpunktnchmen = placing the forefinger round the trigger at the proper point.

Zielen = aiming at the object to be hit.

Abziehen = pressing the trigger (translated in these pages as " pulling off ").— TRANSLATOR.

&c., the dress laid down for preparatory exercises being worn at first.

In practising these forms of the present, great importance is to be attached to rapidity in aiming.

3. Great attention must be devoted to the mode of loading the rifle as a single and multiple loader, as laid down in the Regulations, the learning of which is considerably facilitated by the use of practice ammunition.

4. During this introductory period, aiming ammunition is of great value as a means of instruction. Detailed instructions for its employment are given in a special regulation.

In subsequent stages of the instructional course, this aiming ammunition also forms an excellent means of assistance to bad shots.

5. The firing of blank cartridge forms the final stage in the preparatory instruction for target practice. At first the firing rest will be used, and a target will be aimed at.

6. Firing exercises with ball cartridge will not be begun until the men have attained perfect precision in presenting. At this period the recruit must be instructed in the rudiments of judging distance.

7. In conducting exercises in the present and in firing, the most suitable position for the instructor is generally to the left front of the firer. From this point mistakes made by the latter in position, bearing, position of the rifle, placing the forefinger round the trigger, firing, &c., are most easily observed. It is of course open to the instructor to change that position as may be required.

Faults committed by the firer in presenting will frequently have to be spoken about without letting him bring his rifle down to the "ready," in order that the remarks made may be more convincing and instructive. Such instruction must be given as quietly as possible, but briefly, so that the man may not be over-tired, especially in presenting free-handed.

If the firer becomes unsteady, he must be allowed to come down to the ready, and it may even be necessary to break off the man's shooting altogether for that day.

After the shot has been fired, the man must remain a moment in the position of "present." In this way faults originating in unsteadiness, uncertainty, or dread of fire, will be best checked.

The motion of coming down to the "ready" is to be executed calmly.

After a shot has been fired, the instructor indicates any faults that have been committed, and gives such instruction as may serve to avoid them in future; similarly he explains the external influences which affect the position of the hit, and the precautions which should be taken to counteract them.

8. The rifle cannot be used with effect in the combat unless aptness be acquired in the following matters, which must be incessantly practised; judicious choice of the position to be taken up with reference to the field of fire, taking advantage of

all the circumstances which present themselves on the ground either for steadying the rifle or covering the firer, accurate judging of distances, rapid loading, skilful handling of the magazine loading arrangement, adjusting the sights with rapidity and precision, rapidity and dexterity in coming to the present in every possible position of the body, and quickness in aiming. Practice in each of these branches of duties must never be discontinued for a long time. Especially are practices in aiming and presenting with sights for all distances, and at distances which correspond to the sights used, to be kept up constantly throughout the entire service of the man; the practices, however, should not be continued too long at a time, and should always be interesting and instructive.

Bad shots must be again put through the preliminary exercises. Before they resume their firing exercises, the company chief must personally satisfy himself as to their progress and the adequacy of their preparatory instruction.

§ 16. AIMING.

In aiming, such an elevation and lateral direction must be given to the rifle that the object to be aimed at shall be hit.

1. Elevation is obtained by selecting the sight which corresponds to the distance of the object, and by so bringing the fore-sight into the notch of the back-sight that the firer sees the top of the fore-sight in the middle of the notch and on a level with the shoulders of the back-sight ("level sight").[*]

Correct lateral direction is ensured by having the shoulders of the back-sight horizontal and bringing the line of sight and point to be hit in the same vertical plane.

As the "level sight" (Fig. 11, a) represents only one particu-

FIG. 11.

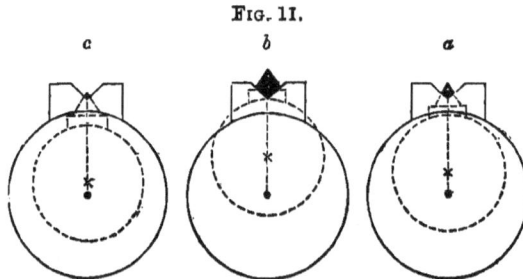

lar and definite manner of taking aim, while every other kind of aim admits of various degrees, the extent to which the fore-sight and notch of the back-sight are above the axis of the barrel is calculated for "level sight." This kind of sight must therefore be used as a rule in aiming.

[*] "*Gestrichen Korn.*" This is termed "fuller sight" in the British Regulations for Musketry Instruction. The above arbitrarily chosen term seems preferable for the purposes of this translation.—TRANSLATOR.

2. The most frequently occurring faults in aiming are as follows :—

a. Taking "full sight" or "fine sight" (Fig. 11, *b* and *c*); the former causes the rifle to shoot high: the latter makes it shoot short.

A well-trained firer may, however, occasionally employ these two kinds of sight intentionally, although they are of themselves faulty, viz., when firing at a small object, in order to obtain a more favourable point to aim at than he would otherwise have.

b. Inclining the sights (turning the barrel round its axis) so that the shoulders of the back-sight are not horizontal, but inclined to one side or the other, that is, canted over. The deviation of the bullet takes place to that side towards which the inclination is given, and moreover the shot will be somewhat short.

c. Clinging of the fore-sight (Kornklemmen). If the tip of the fore-sight is not exactly in the middle of the notch, but to one side of it, a man is said to make his fore-sight cling. If the fore-sight clings to the left (Fig. 12), the bullet will fall too much to the left, and *vice versâ.*

FIG. 12.

The results of errors in aiming will be most clearly illustrated by the following proceeding :—The striker-bolt is taken out of the rifle, a perforated muzzle stopper put in, the weapon laid on a sand-bag, and aim taken with "level sight" at the lower edge of a band target placed about 11 yards from the observer. Next look through the barrel, and, by means of a coloured patch, mark the spot where the axis of the barrel will strike the black band. If now one of the faults in aiming above alluded to be committed, still aiming at the lower edge of the black band, on looking again through the barrel the effect of the error on the shooting will be at once plainly seen.

The influence of light, wind, and weather on the shooting will be explained to the firer in a manner suited to his intellectual capacity.

3. The aiming practices of the recruit are begun by the instructor pointing a rifle which is placed on a sand-bag, and causing the man to indicate the point aimed at. Afterwards the man himself must aim at a given point. Proficiency in aiming can be tested most certainly by pointing the rifle, placed on a sand-bag, at any given point on the target at about 11 yards distance, and ordering the recruit to direct another man, by signs, to move a small paste-board target backward and forward on the target until the line of sight meets the centre of the paste-board target, the latter having a hole in the centre and being attached to the end of a stick. If now the point

aimed at be marked on the large target with the point of a pencil, and this proceeding repeated once or twice without the man moving the rifle, it is not difficult to ascertain, from the greater or less deviation of the two or three points marked on the target, whether and how the man can aim.

As soon as the recruit has acquired a certain facility in aiming with the rifle in a fixed position, he will proceed to aim in free-handed positions, and in these exercises it is advisable to use an aiming apparatus to control the firer.

In free-handed aiming, the rifle will at first be pointed about half a yard below the spot to be aimed at and then gradually raised, while in all other modes of presenting, aim will be taken at once at the point of aim. Having ascertained with both eyes that the shoulders of the back-sight are horizontal, the left eye will be closed, and aiming proper will be commenced. (There are some men who keep both eyes open in aiming, and there is no objection to their doing so.)

In aiming at objects moving in a lateral direction, the man must move his rifle uniformly in the direction in which the object is moving, but in advance of it, due regard being had to the rate of movement and distance of the object. For example, if the target is moving laterally at the rate of 100 metres (109·36 yards) in a minute, he should, in order to hit it, aim a bare man's breadth in advance of it at 100 metres distance, and about $1\frac{1}{2}$ man's breadths at 150 metres.

4. In these exercises the instructor will pay particular attention to the eyesight of the recruits, and at once report any imperfections, with a view to closer investigation being made by the medical officer.

Men who have weak sight of the right eye, but can see well with the left, may aim with the latter.

§ 17. PRESENTING.

In all modes of presenting, the body must be firmly held, but free and unconstrained. Every unnatural contortion of the body, and every excessive exertion, disturbs the steady position of the rifle or makes aiming difficult to the eye. Moreover, badly fitting articles of clothing and equipment interfere with the free use of the rifle.

The soldier must learn to hit not only when shooting slowly, but also during rapid firing.

1. In order to take up the position of "present" standing, with the rifle on the rest, the firer places himself about a pace in rear of the firing rest, turns half-right (raising his rifle), plants his right foot about half a pace to the right on the new front, and places his rifle against the inner side of his right foot, trigger guard to the front.

The knees are pressed back by slightly bracing the calves. Hips and shoulders are turned exactly the same as the feet, so that there is no twisting of the body.

The lower part of the body is not to be drawn in nor the chest thrown forward, neither are the shoulders to be raised. The upper part of the body rests naturally on both hips, and does not project beyond them. The weight of the body is consequently not borne by the balls of the feet only, but equally by the whole surface of the feet, including the heels. The head is turned so far to the left, without the neck being stiff, as to allow of a perfect view of the object.

In order to correct the man's pose, it is a good plan to make him raise his heels, and, as he puts them down again, distribute the weight of his body equally on both legs and both feet. In this position the rifle is brought to the right side of the breast, as in the "ready" in the ranks, so that the lower edge of the butt lies about a finger's breadth above the upper edge of the right pouch, and the rifle is then loaded. After this the right hand grasps the small of the butt so far forward that the forefinger in subsequently pulling off can touch the trigger with the root of the first joint. With this object, when the forefinger is of the usual length, it is to be brought so far within the trigger-guard that the finger nail touches the left edge of the inner surface of the trigger-guard. The remaining fingers are clasped evenly round the small of the butt, so to speak squeezing it or holding it by suction, and as nearly as possible with the thumb close to the front joint of the middle finger. The palm of the hand also adapts itself to the small of the butt as far as the wrist. The right arm lies lightly against the outer side of the butt.

From this position the rifle is raised with both hands so far to the front that the butt does not catch under the arm, and then brought firmly back into the shoulder, chiefly with the right hand, the shoulder itself not being brought forward towards the butt or even raised. At the same time the right elbow is raised to about the same height as the shoulder, the butt resting in the hollow thus formed between the collar and the pad formed by the muscles of the shoulder. It is a serious fault to place the butt against the collar bone or on the muscles of the upper arm.

During the act of raising and drawing in the rifle, the man must breathe lightly, after which the breathing must be restrained until the trigger is pulled.

Taking a fresh hold with the right hand, or easing its hold after coming to the "present," is not allowed.

The rifle, the muzzle of which was somewhat raised when it was placed in the hollow of the shoulder, is now laid on the firing rest, between the upper and middle ring, without pressing on the rest.

Slight differences in height can be compensated for by a somewhat wider or closer position of the feet, by the man pressing forward or drawing further back, but never by raising or lowering the shoulders, bending at the hips, or pushing the upper part of the body forward or backward.

The left hand, with the thumb extended along the stock, the remaining four fingers bent and lightly placed together, supports the rifle with the whole palm of the hand, about under the balance. Men with long arms may place the left hand somewhat further forward, and men with short arms somewhat further to the rear, than the balance.

The left arm directs the rifle on the mark in a perfectly natural position, that is, without the elbow being turned too much to the left or right; and in doing this, the back must not be bent or the hips twisted.

The head, slightly inclined forward, rests lightly on the butt, without the muscles of the neck being strained.

2. The "present" standing, free-handed, is performed in the same way, excepting that the muzzle of the rifle is not raised during the "present," but directed at first about half a metre below the mark.

3. The most advantageous way of aiming at objects in motion—whether lying down, kneeling, behind objects serving for cover, or as a support for the rifle—depends upon the build of the individual firer, the ground, the nature of the object aimed at, and the circumstances of the fight.

Speaking generally, only the following rules can be given:—

a. For certainty and convenience in firing lying down, a support for the rifle is of very great value. Nearly every sort of ground presents suitable objects for supporting the rifle, or the possibility of making them with very little trouble. The side-arm must not be used as a rest for the rifle.

The "present" lying down, with the rifle supported, is, as a rule, executed by the firer lying flat on the ground, somewhat obliquely to the object, with his legs extended and not excessively far apart, and supporting the rifle between the upper and middle ring. In doing this, it is not forbidden to individual men to cross their legs if they can thus get into a position for the present better suited to their build. The rifle is pressed against the shoulder and directed by the left hand, which grasps the butt with the four fingers on the outside and the thumb on the inside.

The body rests on both elbows, and the thumb of the right hand is pressed firmly down on the small of the butt.

For firing at long ranges, in order to admit of the butt being lowered, the rest for the rifle must be correspondingly raised, and, if necessary, the rifle may even be pushed so far to the front as to lie on its support somewhere between the middle and lower ring.

In presenting lying down, free-handed, both elbows are supported on the ground. The left hand grasps the stock in front of the trigger-guard, and supports the rifle from below; while the right hand, grasping the rifle at the small of the butt, presses it to the shoulder, and directs it. In other respects, the position of the body is the same as in the present lying down with a rest.

b. The present kneeling, which position is always to be assumed from the half-right turn, can be executed on one or both knees.

In the present on one knee, the right knee rests on the ground, and the left is bent nearly at right angles. The man fires either free-handed, or resting his left arm on his knee. In the latter case, the right arm presses the butt against the shoulder (or, when very high sights are used, against the breast), the elbow being bent outwards. The last-mentioned mode of presenting, in which no fixed rule for the position of the left hand can be given, is especially to be recommended for long ranges, and must, therefore, be thoroughly familiar to all the men.

In the present on both knees, the latter must be separated as widely as possible. The body may remain erect, or be allowed to sink down behind, in which case either the feet must be crossed, or the heels closed.

c. In the present behind a tree which affords cover from the enemy's fire, the right shoulder will be drawn back as much as possible, the feet assuming a suitable position. In the case of thick trees the left forearm, and in that of smaller ones the palm of the left hand, will be placed against the stem. In the former case, the rifle rests on the palm of the hand; in the latter, between the thumb and forefinger.

d. The present behind a breastwork. The whole of the left side of the body leans against the interior slope of the breastwork, the right foot being drawn back. If there is a step [cut out of the top of the interior slope, Appendix A, Fig. 2] both elbows are to rest upon it, and the rifle, which lies on the crest of the breastwork, will be pressed against the shoulder, as in the present lying down with a rest.

§ 18. PULLING OFF, AND POINT REALLY AIMED AT.

1. The way in which the trigger is pulled back until the shot is fired (*Abziehen*) has an enormous influence on the shooting; it must, therefore, be minutely explained, and constantly practised with the utmost diligence.

Pulling off will at first be demonstrated with a fixed rifle, and the recruit will be taught how the forefinger must be smartly advanced to the trigger with the root of the first joint on it, assume its proper position for pulling off, and by a continuous, gradual, and uniform bending of the two other joints complete the pull off the moment the point to be aimed at is reached. The more the forefinger is curved in pulling off, so much the more necessary is it that the right hand as far as the wrist should remain firmly in contact with the small of the butt. It is only in this way that the motion of the finger is prevented from extending beyond the knuckle, and communicating itself to the whole hand, and so to the arm. It is recommended that the instructor, after the recruit has settled his finger on the trigger, should place his own finger on that of the man, and so illustrate how the trigger should be pulled. Subsequently, the placing of the forefinger in position and pulling off will be practised in the present free-handed. Whether the firer understands properly how to pull off can be ascertained by carefully observing the first joint of the forefinger. During the act of pulling off the right eye remains fixed on the mark, and neither the head, the right shoulder, nor the left hand, should be allowed to move. After the shot is fired, the man holds the trigger back for a moment, states what point he actually aimed at, or believes he has hit, opens the left eye, slowly straightens his forefinger, and comes down to the "ready," at the same time raising his head quietly.

2. If it has been found possible to overcome the difficulties in acquiring a uniform and gradual pull off, these usually reappear, and in increased measure, when blank cartridge, aiming ammunition, and especially ball cartridge are brought into use.

The firer is inclined to be apprehensive lest, after getting his rifle well on to the mark, he should miss the favourable moment for firing if he does not do so immediately. Instead of pulling off calmly, he does so in a hasty manner, with a start —he jerks. Through anticipating the report and recoil which accompany the discharge, the firer is also apt to fall into other faults; he bends his head forward, closes the right eye, brings the right shoulder forward—he "bobs." In both cases, there cannot be any certainty in the firing, or in assigning the position of the hit. These faults of jerking and bobbing cannot always be outwardly detected, indeed, they frequently escape the close observation of the instructor at the moment of firing, and are unnoticed by the firer himself. They are generally not seen plainly until a cartridge misses fire contrary to the expectation of the man. In order that he may be made conscious of the existence of these defects, it is advisable to hand him occasionally a rifle loaded with a miss-fire cartridge, or an unloaded rifle at full cock.

3. Great importance is to be attached to the man reporting correctly the point really aimed at at the moment of firing (*Abkommen*, § 3, 1).

The report "well-aimed," which only leads to inattention, is not to be allowed, and the man is to be urged seriously and patiently, whenever he cannot exactly state the point his line of sight was directed at, to acknowledge it truly by reporting "point really aimed at uncertain," or to that effect. A progressive improvement in shooting is only possible when the instruction imparted inculcates these principles and is conducted with untiring patience, While men of the 3rd musketry class are to be asked the point at which their line of sight was really directed, those of the 1st and 2nd classes are to state the point where they have probably hit the target.

§ 19. Combining the several Operations in Firing.

The several operations of presenting, aiming, and pulling off are combined in the order of their occurrence in the following directions for firing standing free-handed :—

The body turned half-right, the rifle being raised, the right foot placed about half a pace to the right on the new front. The rifle lowered to the inner side of the right foot; weight of the body equally distributed on both legs and on the whole sole of both feet.

The head turned towards the mark. The rifle brought to the "ready" position and loaded. The small of the butt grasped and held by suction.

The rifle raised and at the same time carried slightly forward, and brought in principally by the right hand to the right shoulder, which does not move. In doing this the breathing, both inspiration and expiration, to be easy, after which it is restrained until the shot is fired.

The left hand, in a perfectly natural position, supports the rifle, all unnecessary exertion being avoided. Meanwhile the forefinger of the right hand has been placed on the trigger and assumes the proper feeling of it; the horizontal position of the shoulders of the back-sight is ascertained with both eyes, the left eye closed and aim taken.

In doing this, the rifle is first directed about half a metre below the mark and raised gradually by the left hand only, without any bending of the loins or hips. As soon as the spot to be aimed at is reached, the trigger is pressed, without jerking, by a gradual and almost imperceptible bending of the forefinger, so that the rifle is discharged without the firer knowing exactly when it will go off.

In proceeding thus, even if the shot is unintentionally fired too soon, the bullet will be fairly well placed; whereas if the firer pulls off with a jerk, in order to catch the moment when his rifle is in the proper direction, the position of the shot cannot be reckoned upon.

It is only with a gradual raising of the rifle and similar mode of pulling off that good free-handed shooting is possible.

If the firer passes over the mark when aiming, before his shot is fired, he again lowers the muzzle about half a metre below the mark and repeats the operation described above. By means of practice and attention, the gradual expenditure of power which takes place during the operation of pulling the trigger must be brought into unison with the space of time necessary for raising the rifle. During the act of pulling off, the eye remains fixed on the mark. As soon as the shot is fired, the man announces the point on which his line of sight was actually directed, or the point hit (as the case may be), extends his forefinger, comes down to the "ready," at the same time raising his head, and lowers his rifle.

V.—JUDGING DISTANCE.

§ 20. In General.

Ability to estimate distances correctly is indispensable for officers, non-commissioned officers, and men; on it depends the proper selection of the sights to be used and the point to be aimed at, with which the success of the musketry combat is essentially bound up.

The men must learn to estimate distances up to 400 metres (437·4 yards) with accuracy, and must be practised in judging from 400 to 800 metres (874·9 yards). Officers, non-commissioned officers, and intelligent men ought to be able to judge up to 800 metres, and are to be practised in determining distances between 800 and 1,200 metres (1,312·3 yards). Lastly, officers ought to be able to read distances quickly and accurately from a large scale map, not only from 800 to 1,200 metres, but beyond that.

Judging or finding out distances can be gone about in various ways: either the distance on the surface of the ground is estimated by the eye, in doing which the correct determination of the distance is greatly influenced by the degree of distinctness of the object whose distance has to be ascertained, or the time which elapses between the flash or smoke and the report of a shot is noted, and the distance calculated on the datum that sound travels about 340 metres (371·8 yards) per second. On this fact depend many systems of measuring distances.

The latter mode presupposes that an enemy is firing, and, owing to the difficulty of estimating smaller periods of time than a second with any degree of accuracy, can only be employed for long distances and generally only in the case of artillery fire.

Consequently distances must in most cases be measured by the eye on the ground; and therefore, in exercises for judging distances, special endeavour must be made to attain great accuracy in this respect.

The distances to be estimated should occasionally be marked by men or detachments, in full field service order, lying down, kneeling, or standing.

Men are to judge distance not only when they themselves are standing, but especially when lying down or kneeling.

The exercises must be carried out on ground of varying nature. In addition to the nature of the ground, the influence of the light, the weather, and the time of day must be taken into consideration.

Estimates of distance are generally too short under the following circumstances: in very bright sunshine, in a clear atmosphere, when the sun is at the back of the person judging distance, on uniform plains, across water, when the background is bright, on rising or undulating ground, especially when portions of the ground cannot be seen into. On the contrary, distances are frequently over-estimated in great heat (a gleaming atmosphere), with a dark background, when facing the sun, in dull misty weather, in twilight, in woods, on falling ground, and when the enemy is only partially seen.

Quite apart from the influences above mentioned, distances are generally under-estimated in real warfare.

The actual distance of the objects observed, single men or detachments, must be determined in a trustworthy way by pacing, measuring off with a cord, or, in the case of long distances, by using maps and any distance measures available.

Exercises in the use of the rifle must always go hand-in-hand with judging distance practices.

§ 21. COURSE OF INSTRUCTION.

1. *Preparatory Exercises.*

a. Pacing.—In order to enable non-commissioned officers and men to determine the correctness of estimated distances, they are to be trained to pace accurately. To this end they will pace an accurately measured piece of ground, 100 metres long, using their own ordinary pace, and observe how many of such paces they take to cover the distance. In subsequently measuring distances by pacing, they make a momentary halt every time they have taken the number of paces corresponding to 100 metres, go on counting another 100 metres, and continue the process, being careful to note the number of hundreds of metres which they pass over; for this purpose they can, if necessary, assist themselves by taking down the figures. The distance last paced, if under 100 metres, will be turned into the number of metres corresponding approximately to that of the paces required to cover it. It is best to count double paces in pacing distances.

b. Impressing Units of Measures on the Mind.—The distances 50 and 100 metres are to be marked off in various directions, including lateral lines, and endeavour must be made to accustom the eye to these distances as much as possible. The men must know that lines in a lateral direction appear longer than those which are of the same length but lie directly in front of them, and that lines of a given length appear shorter the further they are off.

In order to test the progress made by the men in impressing on their minds the distances referred to, the instructor orders them to move a given distance along a line, or to describe points on the ground which are 50 or 100 metres from their own position. In each case the accuracy of the estimates formed will be tested by measuring the distance with a cord or by means of previously arranged marks on the ground which are known only to the instructor.

Men will not proceed to further exercises in judging distance until they have learnt to estimate the above distances with accuracy.

2. *Judging Distances up to 200 metres.*

In the case of distances between 100 and 200 metres, it is advantageous to apply by the eye the known units of measure to the distance to be estimated, or to divide the ground by determining a point which lies exactly in the middle, and so calculate the length of half the entire distance.

3. *Judging Distances up to 400 metres.*

a. The observer mentally applies the units of measure known to him to the line leading to the object whose distance is to be estimated ; in the first instance, the larger one of 100 metres repeated, if necessary, and then the smaller one of 50 metres, if it be required.

b. The observer selects a point in the line to be estimated which he considers halves the whole distance, calculates the length of the half lying nearer to him (if necessary again halving it), and doubles or quadruples the resulting measurement.

The mode of procedure mentioned in *a* is very liable to lead to erroneous conclusions in judging long distances, as it is difficult to determine correctly the degree to which a portion of ground appears shorter to the eye than it really is the further it is from the observer. Consequently the method *b* is generally to be preferred.

c. If the ground between the observer and the object whose distance is to be estimated cannot be seen into throughout, or if distances have to be judged on long and uniformly level plains, it may be advantageous to transfer the terminal points of the length to be estimated, by the eye, to side lines, *e.g.*, a row of trees, the edge of a wood, &c., and to judge the distance on such side lines.

In the field, however, it will nearly always be required to judge distances as rapidly as possible on the line lying immediately in front of one, and therefore in all exercises and inspections in judging distance, the greatest importance is to be attached to this way of proceeding.

The rapid judging of distances on a forward line is very much facilitated by the observer so firmly impressing upon his mind distances, not of 100 metres only, but of 200, and even greater extent, that he can mentally convey them with certainty to the ground to be estimated.

Familiar lengths of ground which have to be passed over daily, such as those of the drill ground, barrack yard, or a street, should repeatedly be impressed on the eye as a valuable aid in judging distance on the ground.

4. *Judging Distances up to 800 metres.*

The estimation of these distances, which should only be arrived at gradually, can be made in the same way as laid down under 3. It is facilitated by the attainment of readiness in determining whether the object whose distance is to be judged is under or over 400 metres off. It is also advantageous if the observer can at once judge what is the greatest distance at which the given object can be, and what is the least distance at which it must be. From these two estimates, which however should be kept within the closest limits, a mean can be struck, and the result so arrived at corrected according to circumstances by other observations.

The last stage of instruction consists in exercises in judging whether an object is under or over 800 metres distance; and great readiness must be acquired in this practice.

5. *Judging Distances up to 1,200 metres.*

This is facilitated if distances of 400 and 800 metres are first determined in the direction of the object; in other respects the directions given in 3 and 4 will be carried out.

If the ground cannot be seen into all the way up to the object, the observer, in order to obtain a better view of the ground, may advantageously shift his position to one side, if the circumstances of the combat admit of it, and thence estimate the distance.

VI.—TARGET PRACTICE.

§ 22. OBJECT OF TARGET PRACTICE.

By means of target practice, officers, under-officers, and men should attain to and preserve the highest degree of aptitude in firing, learn how to apply the rules for using the sights and choice of point of aim, and become adept in the use of the rifle in all the firing positions. Important, however, as target practice is of itself, it must not be looked upon as an ultimate object, but merely as a preparatory school for firing under conditions of warfare.

Exercises at the shorter distances are especially useful for training the rifleman in accurate shooting, and consequently a comparatively greater expenditure of time and ammunition over them is thoroughly justifiable.

The gradually progressive training of the men in shooting requires that they should be divided into firing classes; of these three have been established, and special exercises prescribed for each.

§ 23. GENERAL RULES.

1. The musketry year begins on the 1st October of one

(3269)   c year and ends on the 30th September of the following year, after the latter of which it is named.

2. The captain, all the lieutenants, under-officers and privates, take part in the target practices of their company, in so far as they are not prevented from doing so through being "on command," &c.

Officers "on command" as adjutants, &c., in the same garrison as their own corps, will, without exception, be called in for target practice.

3. Every man will, in the course of the current year, shoot off the whole of the exercises laid down for his class. (Compare the introductory remarks to "Firing Exercise Report," Form 3.) It may, therefore, be necessary, due regard being paid to the amount of ammunition at disposal, to let men proceed with the exercises who have failed repeatedly to fulfil the conditions of one or several series.

If, after shooting through all the exercises, any cartridges are still at disposal, or if it can be foreseen during the exercises that there will be a surplus, attempts must be repeated to fulfil the conditions which have been neglected.

In apportioning the number of rounds which can be expended in any exercise before proceeding to the one next following, the company-chief must take into consideration that, for the purpose of ensuring a thorough grounding in musketry, men of the youngest annual class should never commence the principal exercises, if it can be avoided, until they have fulfilled the conditions of the preliminary exercise.

4. Men whose short-sightedness with the right eye is certified by the medical officer, and who for any special reasons cannot aim with the left eye, perform the firing exercises in the same way as the other men, but only at distances for which their sight, if necessary with the aid of spectacles, is adapted. Such men are ineligible for receiving musketry prizes or marksmen's badges, and cannot be promoted into higher musketry classes.

5. In selecting the practice days, it must be borne in mind that unfavourable weather, especially during the instruction of the recruit, has a prejudicial effect. Target practice should never be preceded by violent exercise.

6. Every fore- and after-noon counts as a distinct working day. Rushing through the exercises with undue haste has quite as bad an effect as discontinuing them for any length of time; it may, however, be advisable in the case of individual bad shots, who have lost heart, and whose shooting has not been improved by supplementary practices, to let them give up firing altogether for some time, so that they may have the necessary rest.

7. The uniform to be worn is as follows:

a. For the preliminary practice: Forage cap, belts, 2 front ammunition pouches.

b. For the principal practice: Helmet, chin-straps, raised or under the chin, knapsack loaded to 8·8 lbs., mess tin (carried in the ordinary manner for the line of march), belts, 3 ammunition pouches, and cloak.

Under-officers and men wear the tunic at all firing exercises. It is optional to wear the haversack, and it is left to the corps concerned to decide whether the knapsacks shall be carried loaded on the march to the ranges. Under-officers do not put on the knapsack until they reach the range.

§ 24. SHOOTING CLASSES.

The 3rd shooting class consists of men of the youngest annual class, those who are certified to be short-sighted by the medical officer, and the men of the older annual classes who are not yet classified as trained shots. Completely trained and good shots form the 2nd class, and the 1st class is composed of thoroughly safe marksmen.

As soon as the firing exercise is completed, the company-chief selects the men who are eligible for promotion into the next higher class; those men only being taken into account who have shot through the whole of the practices of the class in question, and fulfilled all the conditions (where such are pre-scribed) without exception. Serious faults which a man cannot get rid of, and which render his permanent reliability in shooting very doubtful, justify a company-chief in postponing his advancement, even if the number of rounds which the man had to fire in order to fulfil the conditions imposed upon his class was comparatively low. It is, moreover, by no means a neces-sary condition that all the men should always be in the class corresponding to their year of service, although this must be zealously striven for.

The Battalion Commander decides as to the distribution of the officers to the musketry classes, according to the pro-posals of the Company Commander.

Officers and under-officers who have twice fulfilled all the conditions of the 1st class form the special shooting class. For this class special exercises are proposed by the Regimental Commander.

The displacement of a man from a higher into a lower class is not permissible; on the contrary, the greatest attention must be paid to men to whom the requirements of the higher class present great difficulties.

Promotion to the next higher shooting class takes place on the termination of a successful course of training at the Military School of Musketry.

A remark will be entered in the discharge papers according to the form used, indicating shooting class, musketry prizes, and marksmen's badges.

§ 25. DUTY WITH THE FIRING DETACHMENT.

1. The musketry under-officer of the company makes all the necessary arrangements for the shooting at the range. He looks after the provision of ammunition, musketry ap-

pliances, targets, writing material, and the "Musketry Regulations," of which there must always be a copy at hand at every exercise at the ranges. He also distributes the fatigue men. His other duties consist in keeping the musketry book and all rolls relating to musketry, keeping in good order all the apparatus required for shooting and the preliminary exercises, and paying special attention to the rifles, ammunition, lead picked up the ranges, and cartridge cases. One of the men, a good on penman, may be temporarily allowed to assist the musketry under-officer in keeping the musketry book and rolls.

2. Privates will be marched to and from the ranges in formed bodies. Before marching off to the ranges, and again shortly before the commencement of the firing, the rifles must be inspected and especial care taken that the barrels are clean and perfectly free from foreign bodies.

Every man must have his musketry small book with him.

3. The superintending staff, which as a general rule will be relieved every two hours, consists of:—

a. The Officer: He is responsible for the conduct of the entire shooting, for the preservation of order at the ranges, and for the observance of the rules for ensuring safety.

If there is only one subaltern officer at the disposal of the company, the company-chief may detail an under-officer with officer's sword-knot to superintend the shooting.

Before the shooting begins, the officer satisfies himself as to the safety of the markers' shelters, the correct placing of the targets, the regulation form of the targets, and the arrangement of the mirrors in the markers' shelters. During the firing, the instruction of the firer, the surveillance of the writer and of the markers specially devolve upon him.

When the firing is finished, the officer will certify the correctness of the shots entered and the number of rounds expended, by his countersignature, and add any remarks that may seem necessary.

In order to check the marking, it is advisable that the officer, some time before the commencement of the firing, should observe the patches on the several parts of the target, and, either during the shooting or after its conclusion, compare these observations and the entries in the musketry book with the bullet holes on the target. The employment of targets which are so riddled as to make such an examination impossible is not permissible.

b. The under-officer superintending the firing: His business is to see that no rifle is loaded before the flag is visible on ranges with markers' shelters of the old sort, or, in the case of ranges with blinded or sunken markers' shelters, so long as the target is invisible or the signalling is not finished. This under-officer also notices the signals of the marker, and takes care that the firer, when the signalling is ended, removes the cartridge case from the rifle and on doing so examines it to see if there are any cracks in it.

If the officer is engaged in superintending the writer, and has not ordered the discontinuance of the shooting, the superintendence of all the proceedings of the firer devolves upon the under-officer.

c. The under-officer or lance-corporal for superintending and issuing ammunition: In addition to the superintendence of ammunition during the shooting, this under-officer directs the working party with the firing detachment, and if necessary looks after the temporary cleaning of the cartridge cases, which is done as far away as possible from the firing detachment.

d. The writer for entering the shots: His place, somewhere near the officer directing the exercise, is so chosen that he can readily distinguish the signals made by the marker. The writer has to observe these signals and to enter the several shots in ink, after the firer has announced them, in the rough musketry practice sheets and in the musketry small books, which are given to him immediately before the shooting begins. At the same time he repeats the name of the firer aloud, and the result of the shot; in doing this it is his duty to at once mention any discrepancies between the firer's announcement and the signals made by the marker. Any intentional error in entering the shots will be dealt with in accordance with § 139 of the "Militär-Strafgesetzbuch."*

4. When at the range, the detachment which is about to shoot, and which as a rule will not exceed 5 men, takes post a few paces in rear of the firing station, opposite the target, with chambers opened and magazines cut off.

From this position each individual firer steps forward, with ordered rifle, assumes the position prescribed for the practice, and loads without word of command and without using the safety bolt, when it is permissible (in accordance with the instructions previously given) to do so. In loading and unloading the magazine, which must only be done at the express instance of the officer, and when the markers are under cover, the firers must front towards the butt. The further procedure with regard to firing is regulated by the rules laid down in §§ 16 to 18.

If the firer comes down to the "ready" before he has fired, without wishing to leave the stand, he leaves his rifle ready to fire; otherwise it must be unloaded.

If a cartridge misses fire, it will in the first instance be turned round in the chamber so as to give it another position. If it still misses fire, it will be loaded in another rifle which is considered to be perfect.

If the cartridge again refuses to explode at first trial in

* § 139 of the "Militär-Strafgesetzbuch" runs as follows:—"Any person who intentionally draws up a false official certificate or renders an incorrect report of any kind, or knowingly transmits such, will be punished with imprisonment from six months to three years, and with reduction to the status of a soldier of the 2nd class. In less serious cases the punishment will be medium or close arrest, or imprisonment or confinement in a fortress not exceeding six months."

this rifle, it will be marked as a " complete miss-fire," and made over to the musketry under-officer.

If a cartridge cannot be loaded owing to abnormal external measurement, or the case is flattened, the detonating-cap wanting, &c., it is marked as " unserviceable," and returned. In both cases an entry is made in the rough musketry practice sheet, and in the musketry book. The same is done if it is seen after firing that a cartridge case has split length- or cross-wise. As soon as the shot has been signalled, the firer announces the result, at the same time giving his name. He then removes the case from the chamber, examines it for any cracks, and returns to his original place. This, however, is not to prevent his firing several shots in succession when firing kneeling, lying down, or behind a parapet.

When firing at disappearing targets, the firer comes to the "present" the moment he sees the target appear; in this case he loads as soon as the target is drawn under cover after the shot has been signalled, or as soon as the flag is shown.

5. No firer is allowed to fulfil more than two conditions on one and the same working day. On the other hand, he should not as a rule fire less than 5 cartridges (3 in the preliminary practice) in one working day.

The supplementary issue of cartridges is regulated by the company-chief, with the restriction that more than 3 rounds in the preliminary practices, or 5 in the principal practices, should only exceptionally be issued as a supplementary allowance, and then only for the special purpose of fulfilling a condition.

If the condition attached to any particular practice is to be fulfilled, the last (5 or 3) shots fired on one and the same working day are to be taken for the fulfilment of the condition ; thus, for example, if 6 rounds are expended, the condition is to be fulfilled with the second (or fourth) to the sixth shot.

If a condition is fulfilled with less than 5 (or 3) rounds, 5 (or 3) cartridges are nevertheless to be fired. It is absolutely forbidden to allow individual bad shots to fulfil all the conditions of their class by making them a supplementary issue of ammunition out of reasonable proportion.

In firing at disappearing targets, the fact of omitting to fire is not to be considered a fault.

It is forbidden to attain apparently better results by providing special facilities which have a prejudicial effect on the training of the men for actual warfare, such as putting particular marks on the targets ; on the other hand, it is permitted to make use of screens. The use of aiming apparatus for controlling the firer is not allowed in target practice.

§ 26. DUTY AT THE TARGET.

The markers, consisting of an under-officer or lance-corporal and the necessary fatigue men, are taken from the company which is firing. The markers are not to act as such for more than two hours in succession, and are neither to wear light-coloured nor red jackets.

On ranges of the old sort, and those which have blinded markers' shelters, the markers of one range are forbidden to communicate with those of a neighbouring one.

The under-officer or lance-corporal is responsible for the most careful observance of the rules for avoiding accidents at the target, for the correct placing of the latter and of the mirror arrangement, for the proper movement of disappearing targets, for the conscientious noting and signalling of the shots, and for the careful closing of the bullet holes. Inaccurate marking, if intentional, is punishable under § 139 of the Militär-Strafgesetzbuch. Every year, before the firing practices begin, the company-chiefs are to instruct and warn under-officers and men as to the offence of false marking.

The target is placed as near as possible to the butt, perpendicularly on the ground, or on the sill, carriage, tram, &c., provided for it, and at right angles to the central line of the range.

Disappearing targets remain visible for five seconds only, that is, the length of time necessary for counting nine at the usual rate of marching.

If a shot strikes the dividing line between two rings, the higher number is considered to be hit. A similar rule holds good if the band, man's-breadth, figure, or any part of the equipment is struck.

In the case of oblique hits, the bullet hole is merely covered with the marking stick, and the shot signalled as a " miss."

The duty of the markers varies according to the kind of marker's shelter used. It is regulated as follows :—

1. *On Ranges with Markers' Shelters of the Old Pattern.*

When the firing is to begin, as soon as the markers have got inside the shelter, a red and white stiff flag or panel of suitable size is shown from the shelter at the side of the target so as to be seen by the firing detachment.

The further proceedings depend upon whether the markers are to signal after each shot or only after a certain number of shots has been fired.

In the former case, if the superintending marker has observed by means of the mirror that a shot has fallen on the range, and if the markers have observed the impact of the bullet on the target or in its immediate vicinity, they slowly withdraw the flag and leave the shelter; in any other case the markers are not to leave the shelter unless a man brings them the order to do so or the signal to cease firing is given by the firing detachment.

The marker searches for the bullet hole, marks it with a lead-pencil, and then places himself, while the shot is being signalled, at the side of the target, fronting towards the firing detachment. The bullet hole is to be clearly indicated; the signals for communicating the hits must be as simple as possible, easily distinguished, and made more slowly as the distance is greater. The service of marking at the targets is to be made the subject of special exercises at the beginning of every fresh musketry year, and these exercises must be frequently repeated during the year.

If a bullet hits during the firing at a disappearing target, the target must be made visible to the firer; and not till that is done is the result to be signalled.

As soon as the signalling is finished, the markers betake themselves quickly to the shelter without waiting for any further signal from the firing detachment. The flag will then be again displayed.

For the purpose of examination, the hole made by the last shot always remains open. Thus, if the first shot was a hit, the hole is not to be covered until the next shot has been fired and just before the hole made by the latter is marked with pencil.

For the information of the firer, a mill-board disc, about the same size as the "12," coloured white on one side and black on the other, can be fastened by means of a plug or small hook in the hole made by the last shot. The employment of this disc when firing at the figure target or its modifications is prohibited.

If the marking is not to be signalled after each shot, but only when a certain number of shots has been fired, the flag is first waved twice up and down, and then slowly withdrawn; the shelter may be left half a minute later in a circumspect manner. (If signals are agreed upon (§ 27, 3) it is advisable that the signal for "cease firing" should be given when the fixed number of shots has been fired by the firing detachment.)

When the firing is executed against a fixed target, two markers, in addition to the under-officer or lance-corporal, are sufficient: one of these works the flag, which, as a general rule, he should constantly retain in his hand, while the other attends to the closing of the bullet holes. For working disappearing targets, a third man is requisite.

2. On Ranges with Blinded Markers' Shelters.

The shooting may begin as soon as the target is made visible or the signalling is finished; consequently it is forbidden for the markers to move on the range, or to expose any part of their bodies outside the shelter, from the moment the target is made visible until the shooting is finished—special circumstances excepted, in which it is necessary to break off the firing.

The superintending marker is responsible for watching the range by means of the mirror, marking the bullet holes with a pencil mark, and indicating them with a marker's rod.

One marker moves the carriage which carries the target, another closes the bullet holes, while the third extends and withdraws the panels which show the number of points, according to the instructions of the under-officer.

If the marking is to be done after each shot, the target is withdrawn into the shelter after the first shot, and the bullet hole is sought for and marked with a pencil. Next, the result is signalled by means of the panels of the signal box, the target is again made visible to the firing detachment, the situation of the hit shown by covering the bullet hole with the marker's rod or mill-board disc, and then the rod and signalling panel withdrawn.

This proceeding is repeated for each succeeding shot, with the addition that the man who covers up the bullet holes closes the hole made by the last shot but one as soon as the target is drawn into the shelter, and before the hole made by the last shot is marked with pencil.

Misses are signalled by an up and down motion of the marker's rod.

If the signalling is not done after each shot, but only after a certain number of shots, the target is not drawn into the shelter until the fixed number of shots has been fired.

If, in exceptional cases, it is necessary for the men at the target to leave the shelter, the target is drawn into it, a special signal, previously agreed upon for this purpose, is made with the signalling apparatus, and it is observed by means of the mirror whether this signal is understood by the firing detachment and answered by a counter-signal and the suspension of the firing.

If it is impossible to withdraw the target owing to any hitch, the above signal must be constantly repeated until the attention of the firing detachment is gained and it is acknowledged by a counter-signal or by sending a man; the range may then be cautiously crossed.

When the derangement has been rectified, the target is not to be made visible to the firing detachment until all the markers are again under shelter.

As soon as the marker observes in the mirror the signal to cease fire, he sees that the target is drawn into the shelter.

3. On Ranges with Sunken Markers' Shelters.

The duty of the markers is pretty nearly the same as on ranges provided with blinded markers' shelters.

One man looks after the apparatus for moving the target, another closes the bullet holes, a third raises and lowers the panels used for signalling the hits, while a fourth watches the range by means of the mirror.

In other respects the proceedings are regulated as laid down in sub-paragraph 2, so far as applicable.

Misses are signalled by waving the marker's rod right and left.

In the ranges appropriated to one and the same body of troops, if it can possibly be arranged, only one of the three kinds of markers' shelters is to be used.

If, however, shelters on the old plan are used in conjunction with covered or sunken ones, the service will be carried out in respect of the latter two kinds as described in sub-paragraphs 2 and 3, in addition to which the red and white frame-flag is to be used according to the directions given in sub-paragraph 1.

§ 27. MEASURES OF SECURITY.

In addition to the measures prescribed above, the following precautions will be taken to prevent accidents :—

1. All personal communication between the firing detachment and the markers is to be held on the range itself in the case of ranges with markers' shelters of the old kind and blinded shelters ; in the case of ranges with sunken shelters, the specially constructed communicating ways are to be used.

2. All shouting during the firing exercises is forbidden. Under no circumstances is anything to be shouted to the markers by the firing detachment.

3. In order to save time it is permissible on commencing and ceasing firing or changing the target, and for a few other purposes, to make use of certain special signals by means of flags, the meaning of which must be entered on boards, of which one will be in the markers' shelter and another in the possession of the writer.

4. The employment of the bugle or drum is forbidden.

5. It is not permissible to fire simultaneously on several lines on the same range.

6. Loaded rifles, and those with filled magazines, must never be allowed to leave the hand. The chambers of rifles which are not retained in the hand are always to be open.

7. Aiming and presenting exercises are not to be performed on the ranges.

8. On the conclusion of the firing, barrels and magazines of rifles, and the ammunition pouches of all the men, must be inspected, and a report thereon made to the superintending officer.

9. If the signalling is not to take place after every single shot, but only after a series has been fired, the markers are to be informed in good time and to be warned to be especially cautious.

10. When shooting at distances over 400 metres (437·4 yards), the immediately contiguous ranges must be cleared if the walls separating the ranges in a longitudinal or oblique direction have not a greater height than that prescribed for ordinary circumstances. In the case of ranges with a minimum interval of 32·8 yards from centre to centre, it is not necessary to clear the adjoining ranges when shooting at distances over 400 metres, if there are plantations of sufficient density and height between the ranges.

11. According to local circumstances, the above regulations must be supplemented by special instructions to meet the

requirements of particular ranges. To this end the troops, in concert with the local commandants (senior officers of garrisons), determine in the case of each individual range whether any additional measures of safety, beyond those prescribed above, are necessary, such as posting sentries, prohibiting firing on adjoining ranges at distances of and under 400 metres, limiting the search for spent bullets to certain times, closing existing thoroughfares. Such special regulations are to be permanently posted on a board at the entrance to the range in question.

§ 28. Choice of Sights and Point to be Aimed at.

The point blank range with the standing sight is 200 metres (218·7 yards), with the small flap 300 metres (328 yards), and in the case of the remaining sights, the distance, approximately, for which they are numbered. In addition to the peculiarities of the rifle itself, the choice of the sight to be used must be regulated according to the influence of the atmosphere and the quality of the ammunition, and the firer must always select the sight which enables him to make the best shooting at the target fired at. He must endeavour to hit that part of the object which, taking into consideration its vertical and lateral extent, offers the surest chance of success. The point to be aimed at must therefore be sought for at, below, or above, the spot which it is desired to hit, and the rifle held higher, lower, or to one side, according to the observations made.

The smaller the object is, the more necessary will be the careful observance of the preceding directions.

Aiming Table.

The following data regarding the mean heights of trajectory are founded on a year's shooting with fresh powder M/71, and correspond to the mean annual temperature :—

Sight.	Distance in metres and yards.	Mean height of trajectory in centimetres and inches.	Point to be aimed at on the ring target.
Standing sight ..	50 metres. (54·6 yards.)	+ 24 cm. (9 ·4 in.)	Just above lower cross-patch.
,, ...	100 (109 ·3)	+ 34 (13 ·38)	Just below lower cross-patch.
,, ...	150 (164)	+ 27 (10 ·62)	Just above lower cross-patch.
,, ...	200 (218 ·7)	±0	Centre.
,, ...	225 (245 ·4)	− 21 (8 · 26)	Just below upper cross-patch.
,, ...	250 (273 ·4)	− 49 (19 · 28)	A handsbreadth above the upper cross-patch.

Sight.	Distance in metres and yards.	Mean height of trajectory in centimetres and inches.	Point to be aimed at on the ring target.
Small flap	200 metres. (218·7 yards)	+81 cm. (31·88 in.)	Lower edge of target.
,, ...	225 (245·4)	+70 (27·55)	Ditto.
,, ...	250 (273·4)	+53 (20·86)	A good handsbreadth below lower cross-patch.
,, ...	300 (328)	±0	Centre.
,, ...	325 (355·3)	−36 (14·17)	Just above upper cross-patch.
,, ...	350 (382·7)	−79 (31·09)	Close below upper edge of target.
400 m. sight	300 (328)	+136 (53·54)	——
,, ...	325 (355·3)	+111 (43·69)	——
,, ...	350 (382·7)	+79 (31·09)	Lower edge of target.
,, ...	400 (437·4)	±0	Centre.
450 m. sight	450 (492·1)		
500 ,, ...	500 (546·8)	±0 approximately	Centre.
550 ,, ...	550 (601·4)		
600 ,, ...	600 (656·1)		

§ 29. EXERCISES OF THE THREE CLASSES.

The target practice for each class is divided into preliminary and principal practices.

In the preliminary practices, the elementary principles of musketry are to be learnt at short distances, and the men are to be accustomed to firing with the greatest accuracy, all the rules of musketry being most carefully observed. They will only fire standing with rest and standing with hands free, as these modes of presenting best enable the instructor to observe each separate movement of the firer.

In the principal practices, all that has been learnt during the preliminary practices will be applied to shooting against targets which more or less reproduce the conditions of warfare, and this in various positions of the "present" and at great distances. The firer will be further trained in the use of the magazine attachment, ball cartridges being used, and in accurate shooting.

The bayonet will not be fixed in any of these practices.

THIRD SHOOTING CLASS.

No. of Practice.	Approximate Range in Yards.	Position.	Target.	Conditions to be fulfilled.	Remarks.
				Preliminary Practices (Conditions to be fulfilled in 3 Shots).	
1	110	Standing, with rest	Band target	3 hits in the man's breadth, 1 in the band.	
2	110	Ditto	Ditto	3 hits in the man's breadth, 2 in the band, 1 of them in bull's eye.	
3	110	Ditto	Ring target	3 hits in the man's breadth, 2 in the bull's-eye, 27 points in the rings.	
4	110	Standing, hands free	Ditto	3 hits in the man's breadth, 21 points in the rings.	
5	165	Standing, with rest	Ditto	3 hits in the man's breadth, 1 bull's-eye, 20 points in the rings.	
6	165	Standing, hands free	Ditto	3 hits, 2 in the man's breadth, 15 points in the rings.	
				Principal Practices (Conditions to be fulfilled in 5 Shots; in the last Practice in 6).	
7	165	Lying down, hands free	Body figure	3 hits.	
8	165	Lying down, with rest	Breast figure	3 hits.	
9	220	Kneeling	Kneeling figure	2 hits.	
10	220	Standing, with rest, behind a parapet	Disappearing body figure	2 hits.	
11	275	Lying down, hands free	Full figure	2 hits.	
12	440	Lying down, with rest	Section target	4 hits.	
13	165	Standing, hands free	Ring target	5 hits, 3 in the man's breadth, 1 bull's-eye, 30 points in the rings.	
14	165	Ditto	4 figure targets, 15·7 inches apart.	No conditions. One hit in each of 3 figures is sufficiently good.	1 cartridge in the barrel, 5 in the closed magazine. One minute at the outside allowed (from the first shot) for firing all the cartridges. Magazine fire.

SECOND SHOOTING CLASS.

Preliminary Practices (*Conditions to be fulfilled in 3 Shots*).

No. of Practice.	Approximate Range in Yards.	Position.	Target.	Conditions to be fulfilled.	Remarks.
1	110	Standing, with rest	Band target	3 hits in the man's breadth, 2 in the band in the bull's-eye.	
2	165	Ditto	Ring target	3 hits in the man's breadth, 1 in the bull's-eye, 25 points in the rings.	
3	165	Standing, hands free	Ditto	3 hits in the man's breadth, 15 points in the rings.	

Principal Practices (*Conditions to be fulfilled in 5 Shots; in the last Practice in 7*).

No. of Practice.	Approximate Range in Yards.	Position.	Target.	Conditions to be fulfilled.	Remarks.
4	110	Lying down, with rest	Head figure	3 hits.	
5	165	Lying down, hands free	Breast figure	2 hits.	
6	220	Standing, with rest, behind a parapet	Disappearing breast figure	2 hits.	
7	330	Lying down, hands free	Double figure target	3 hits.	2 figure targets close together.
8	550	Kneeling	Section target	3 hits.	
9	220	Standing, hands free	Ring target	5 hits, 3 in the man's breadth, 25 points in the rings.	
10	165	Kneeling	4 kneeling figures 15·7 inches apart	No conditions. One hit in each of 3 figures is sufficiently good.	1 cartridge in the barrel, 6 in the closed magazine. One minute at the outside allowed (from the first shot) for firing all the cartridges. Magazine fire.

First Shooting Class.

No. of Practice.	Approximate Range in Yards.	Position.	Target.	Conditions to be fulfilled.	Remarks.
				Preliminary Practices (Conditions to be fulfilled in 3 Shots).	
1	110	Standing, with rest	Band target	3 bull's-eyes with 2 hits in the band, or 3 hits in the band with 2 bull's-eyes.	
2	165	Ditto	Ring target	3 hits in the man's breadth, 2 bull's-eyes, 27 points in the rings.	
3	165	Standing, hands free	Ditto	3 hits in the man's breadth, 1 bull's-eye, 21 points in the rings.	
				Principal Practices (Conditions to be fulfilled in 5 Shots; in the last Practice in 9).	
4	165	Lying down, with rest	Head figure	3 hits.	
5	220	Standing, with rest, behind a parapet	Disappearing breast figure	2 hits.	
6	330	Lying down, hands free	2 kneeling figures close together	3 hits.	
7	385	Kneeling	2 figure targets close together	3 hits.	
8	660	Ditto	Section target	3 hits.	
9	220	Standing, hands free	Ring target	5 hits, 4 in the man's breadth, 25 points in the rings.	
10	165	Lying down, hands free	4 body figures, 15·7 inches apart	No conditions. One hit in each of 3 figures is sufficiently good.	1 cartridge in the barrel, 8 in the closed magazine. One minute at the outside allowed (from the first shot) for firing all the cartridges. Magazine fire.

§ 30. TRIAL SHOTS.

In cases in which bad shooting is attributed to the faulty construction of a rifle, the officer conducting the exercises may, for the purpose of testing the weapon, either fire a few shots (termed "trial shots") or cause them to be fired.

The total number will be entered in the rough musketry practice sheets, in the company musketry book, and in the return of ammunition.

§ 31. MUSKETRY PRIZES AND SHOOTING BADGES.

In order to stimulate the zeal of under-officers and men, and to distinguish the good shots, musketry prizes and shooting badges are awarded.

Each battalion receives annually 14 prizes in the shape of silver medals of the total value of £4 5s. 6d.

The medals are sent regularly to the several corps by the General Military Treasury on the 1st August of each year.

(a.) For the under officers of the battalion :—

1. Prize worth 9s.
2.   ,,   4s. 6d.

The former is for under-officers who are in the "special class;" the latter for under-officers who are in the first shooting class.

(b.) For the privates of each company :—

1. Prize worth 7s. 6d.
2.   ,,   6s.
3.   ,,   4s. 5d.

The 1st prize is for the 1st shooting class, the 2nd and 3rd for the 2nd and 3rd classes. If one class fails to make use of its prize, the latter, both in the cases of under-officers and men, passes to the next lower class. Competing under-officers and men must have shot through all the series of their shooting class and completed the practices for which conditions are prescribed. The 1st or 2nd prize is given to such of them as have completed the practices for which conditions are prescribed with the smallest number of rounds, or, in the case of men who have expended the same number of cartridges, have hit the greatest number of man's breadths and figures; if the number of man's breadths and figures is equal, the decision is made according to the number of rings hit. Men who gain medals receive a certificate from the officer commanding the regiment.

Men who are classified as soldiers of the 2nd class have no claim to musketry prizes.

The shooting badge is granted annually to 12 privates in each company, viz., to five men of the 1st class, four of the 2nd, and three of the 3rd. It is awarded on the same principles as laid down for the allotment of musketry prizes. If there are not five privates in the 1st shooting class, the number wanting may be made up from men of the 2nd class who have proved themselves fit for promotion to the 1st class.

Similarly 12 marksmen's badges are given annually to the under-officers of a battalion who are in the special class and 1st class. The distribution to the two classes is regulated according to the number of competitors, with the proviso that only those under-officers of the 1st class can receive the badge whose shooting is not inferior to that of the privates of the 1st class who have not obtained a badge.

Under-officers who have only been promoted to that rank in the course of the musketry year are classed with the privates in respect of competitions for musketry prizes and shooting badges.

Under-officers and privates of the Landwehr district commands are granted shooting badges on the following conditions :—They must have satisfied all the conditions of their shooting class and reached a standard which would have ensured their gaining a badge in a battalion or company of the line regiment bearing the same number, or of the line unit which under § 2, 6, of the "Landwehr-Ordnung" is concerned with the military training of the volunteers of the Landwehr district command.

Reduction to the status of a 2nd class soldier disqualifies a man for earning or retaining a shooting badge, but such disqualification is removed on the man's restoration to the 1st class.

§ 32. Special Exercises for Officers.

Nothing makes a greater impression on the men, or has a better influence on their musketry instruction, than the ability of the officer to illustrate the latter practically in his own person, and to serve as a model to his men.

Opportunity must therefore be given to the officer to perfect his shooting powers in a special manner, outside the routine company exercises.

The battalion commander will call the officers together several times during the best season of the year for practice in shooting with precision, and so direct the exercises in a voluntary way—allowing special targets and private fire-arms to be used—as to engender a liking for shooting and steadily to improve the powers of the officers as marksmen.

It is open to the battalion to institute a special firing register for these practices, but they are not to be entered in the company musketry books.

VII.—FIRING UNDER CONDITIONS OF WARFARE (FIELD FIRING).

§ 33. Object and Division of the Exercises.

Firing under conditions of actual warfare is the ultimate object of the entire musketry instruction, and forms, therefore, the most important portion of it.

It should afford officers, under-officers, and men, the opportunity to perfect their shooting powers and to apply them under circumstances which approach as nearly as can be the conditions of real warfare. For the officers and under-officers, however, the main point is their instruction and practice in the duties which devolve upon them as leaders of companies, züge, or groups; for the men, training in fire discipline.

As the efficiency of the troops is founded on the careful education of each individual man, and the training must proceed gradually from that which is simple to that which is more difficult, field firing is divided into individual firing and firing by formed bodies (groups, half züge or züge of war strength, or larger bodies).

Of the 45 rounds reserved for field firing, 15 are to be used for individual firing and 30 for the firing by formed bodies.

§ 34. Participation in, and Mode of Conducting, the Exercises.

1. All subaltern officers, under-officers, and men take part in the individual firing exercises; in the firing by formed bodies all the under-officers (if it can possibly be arranged) and all the men are to be employed with rifles; the former, when acting as riflemen, may be combined to form separate detachments.

2. An officer is always to direct the exercises with ball cartridge, it being forbidden to replace him by a sword-knot under-officer. Individual and group firing, as well as firing by half-züge of war strength, is carried out under company control; the company chief or battalion commander directs the shooting of züge of war strength, and regimental or battalion commanders direct that of companies on the same footing.

As a rule, the officers and under-officers of the company concerned are present at the shooting of half-züge; in the case of züge and companies, the officers of the battalion.

3. The dress to be worn is the same as directed for the principal exercises in target practice, with the addition of havresac, water-bottle, and entrenching tools. In exercises under conditions of siege warfare, the dress is forage cap, three ammunition pouches, knapsack straps with bag, greatcoat worn over the shoulder and breast, with the mess-tin attached

to it, havresac, water-bottle, and entrenching tools. Bayonets are not fixed.

4. Individual and group firing is executed in the field or on the ranges. In the latter case, the appearance of the range is to be varied by brushwood, &c. The firing of stronger detachments will be carried out in the field only. Special care must be exercised in the selection of the ground, with a view to preventing accidents during the exercises. While the firing is going on, the ground in 'the direction of the shots must be guarded to the extreme range of the rifles, or, in case of the dangerous space being defined by sloping ground or woods, to the confines of the latter. Similarly, suitable measures must be taken to render the ground safe for 500 or 600 metres (say, 550 to 650 yards) to the right and left of the extreme flank lines of fire.

If the exercises are conducted on the ranges, it must be clearly settled whether firing is allowable on the adjoining ranges, and whether any, and if so what, further measures are to be taken to ensure the safety of traffic near the range.

If immunity from danger for the ground on either side and in rear of the butts is not secured by the construction of the range itself, steps must be taken to ensure it as far as the limits above mentioned. When sentry-posts are established to stop the traffic, their safety must be borne in mind. If the markers cannot be provided with sufficient shelter in the neighbourhood of the target, they must be drawn back as far as the firing detachment.

A. INDIVIDUAL FIELD FIRING.

§ 35. FIRE EFFECT.

If the rifle is properly used, it may be considered that there is a probability of each shot hitting under the following circumstances :—

Within 200 metres (218·7 yards) against all objects.

Up to 250 metres (273·4 yards) against a single man kneeling.

Up to 350 metres (382·7 yards) against a file kneeling (two men close together).

Up to 450 metres (492·1 yards) against a group (at least three men) standing, or a single horseman.

If the sight to be used and the spot to be aimed at can be exactly ascertained beforehand, the last two distances may be extended to 400 or 600 metres (437·4 or 656·1 yards) respectively.

The regulations for target practice give the necessary indications as to the employment of sights and the selection of points of aim.

(3269)

D 2

§ 36. Preparatory Exercises.

The exercises with ball cartridge are to be led up to in such a way, by means of instruction in the theory of musketry and demonstrations of the capabilities of the rifle, by exercises in judging distance, and training, hand in hand therewith, in the use of the weapon with practice and blank ammunition, that the only real novelty in the field firing shall be the effect produced by the bullets

The arrangement and course of the preparatory exercises are as follows:—The instructor posts individual men, files, or groups, concealed at certain spots in the drill-ground or in the field, the distances of which are known to him, and directs them to show themselves as targets on his making particular signals agreed upon beforehand; he also instructs them how they are to appear (lying down, kneeling, standing, or in movement; how long they are to remain visible, whether they are to fire blank cartridge, &c.). The inequalities of the ground, brushwood, and groups of trees, are to be intelligently utilised by the men who represent the object. In place of men, targets may be used; but their appearance and manner of moving are generally less in keeping with that which happens in real warfare.

The instructor causes an object to appear, on which the man under instruction must make skilful use of the ground both for getting cover and supporting his rifle, which will be loaded with blank cartridge. The instructor criticises the position taken up and the manner in which it was occupied, from the point of view that all considerations as to cover must give place to such as regard fire-effect. If the position selected by the man is unsuitable, it will be corrected in accordance with the indications given by the instructor.

The man now judges the distance, decides whether he will fire, and (after his estimate of the distance has been corrected, if necessary, by the instructor) states what sight he will use, and the point he will aim at; he then presents, aims, and fires. It must be observed that, in order to strengthen the man's confidence in his skill as a marksman and in his weapon, the shot should be fired, as a rule, only at a distance within the limits at which a hit is probable, and on this point the firer must be thoroughly instructed. This, of course, is not intended to prevent objects being made to appear at distances beyond such limits, with the view of exercising the man's power to make up his mind how he will act. The way in which each action is performed is to be criticised before proceeding further. If the firer has already acquired considerable skill, the instructor allows him to act independently on the appearance of the object, and does not discuss his several proceedings until the shot has been fired.

In the first instance, the use of the standing sight will be taught; afterwards the man will be instructed as to the employment of the higher sights.

These exercises embrace instruction in the utilisation of the ground, judging distance, loading, choice of sights, selection of exact point to be aimed at, presenting, aiming, and firing, and demand high qualifications on the part of the instructional staff. It is therefore necessary that officers and under-officers should be properly trained to direct these exercises. As, moreover, the careful and thorough instruction of the man can only be ensured by not hurrying him on too rapidly, a comparatively long period of time must be set apart for these exercises. The trouble and time devoted to this part of the course will not fail to repay themselves in the subsequent stages of instruction in field firing.

In the case of the men of the youngest annual class, the above exercises are to be begun towards the end of the recruits' period of instruction; in the case of the men of the other annual classes, the exercises are to be carried out without intermission.

§ 37. Exercises with Ball Cartridge.

The exercises are carried out against figure targets and their several modifications, and against targets representing horsemen. With regard to the course to be pursued, the principles laid down for the preparatory exercises are applicable.

For the more advanced marksmen, exercises of the more difficult kinds are to be selected, and special importance is to be attached to the ability to take advantage of brief periods of time during which the target is visible, or the firer leaves cover for the purpose of firing. The value of the exercise will be materially enhanced and interest awakened by varying the distances, the objects (targets on the move, behind gaps or trees, in shelter-trenches, &c.) and the modes of presenting. The magazine is to be completely filled, but not used.

In order that the thorough instruction of the men in the most minute details and careful individual supervision may be possible, it is necessary to make them fire one after the other.

Each man either fires from the same spot at several objects which appear in succession at different distances, or he changes his position by advancing or retiring under the guidance of the officer, &c., conducting the exercise. The possibility of observing the effect of fire which is allowed by exercises with ball cartridge, as distinguished from the preparatory exercises, must be taken advantage of, and another man must accompany the firer, taking up a position near him, observing the effect of his shot, and communicating it to him. In this way not only are the two men who form a file taught to work together, but the habit of observing the effect of fire, which is so important, and only to be acquired by much practice, is impressed upon them.

The hits made by each man are to be noted. In the musketry sheet of the musketry book only the days are entered on which the man was detailed for individual field firing; in the rough musketry practice sheets, however, the name of the man and the number of rounds fired by him on the practice day are to be stated. The company chief determines whether, and in what form, the resulting hits are to be entered in these sheets.

The importance of the exercises forbids that all the cartridges reserved for individual firing should be expended by the man on one day; they ought, indeed, to be divided between at least two days' exercises. The men of the youngest annual class will proceed to practise individual firing with ball cartridge as soon as they have completed the greater part of the principal practices; officers, under-officers, and old soldiers will commence the exercises as soon as possible after the beginning of the new musketry year.

B. FIELD FIRING BY FORMED BODIES.

§ 38. FIRE EFFECT.

In the firing by formed bodies, the bullets spread over an elongated surface, being closer together in the middle than at the ends (§ 6, 6).

Under ordinary circumstances, when the 400 metres sight or one of the higher sights is used, and the ground is parallel to the line of sight, this space—the space covered by fire (*gedeckte Raum* = "beaten zone")—begins and ends about 50 metres (54·6 yards) in front and the same distance beyond the point blank range. Two sights differing by 100 metres cover a space (beaten zone) of 200 metres.

If the fire is directed upon ground rising or falling in relation to the line of sight, the length of the beaten zone will be diminished or increased according to the angle between the line of sight produced and the surface of the ground at the object. In all cases, however, the probability of bringing the cone of fire to bear upon the object remains the same. The fire effect on the object itself in the case of line objects (troops in line) is the same whether the lines are on ground parallel to the line of sight, or rising or falling with regard to it. In the case of column objects (troops in column), however, the fire effect on the object varies: that is to say, columns on ground which rises in relation to the line of sight at any of the ordinary slopes suffer heavier losses than they would on ground parallel to or falling away from the line of sight.

The effect of the fire of formed bodies diminishes as the distance increases, and, apart from the latter consideration and that of the position of the object within the beaten zone, depends chiefly upon the height, breadth, depth, and compactness of the object, and upon the more or less correct estimate of the atmospheric influences.

At short distances, the bullets which pass close above the

heads of the leading body of a company column do not endanger the safety of the rear bodies of the column; at greater distances, however, owing to the increasing curvature of the trajectories, the rear bodies are in danger. Considered, therefore, from a purely theoretical point of view, columns at distances over 800 metres (875 yards) will be in considerably greater danger than troops of the same strength formed in line.

Against low objects, successful results may be expected at short distances, *i.e.*, up to 400 metres (437·4 yards); but at distances over 400 metres, decisive effect can only be obtained by a considerable expenditure of ammunition. High objects can still be fired at with good effect at moderate distances, *i.e.*, from 400 to 800 metres.

Fire at long distances, *i.e.*, over 800 metres, requires the expenditure of a considerable amount of ammunition in comparison with the probable results, and should therefore be employed only in exceptional cases against objects which, owing to their height, and extent of front and depth, present favourable surfaces.

The more the fire is concentrated, both as to time and object, the greater is its moral effect on the bearing of the adversary.

Under certain circumstances, useful effect may be obtained against an object entirely hidden from view. Such fire is termed indirect, and in employing it it is necessary, in order that the object hidden from the firer may be hit, to select a definite point (line) between the firing detachment and the object, as an auxiliary object. As, however, in employing it the properties of the trajectory must be taken into consideration and certain data must be known, in order that the proper sights may be used, indirect firing promises no results on the open field of battle; on the other hand, it may be employed with some effect in fortress warfare when circumstances are favourable, and if special posts are established which can observe the fall of the bullets, and inform the firing detachment accordingly.

FIG. 13.

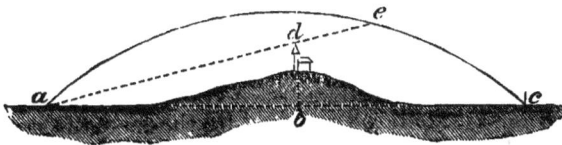

Thus, in Fig. 13, in order that the invisible object *c* may be hit, and the adjustment of the sights *a e* necessary for this purpose may be found, *a c*, *b c*, and *b d* must be known.

frontage, and density, hold out reasonable prospect of favourable results.

A too frequent change of object leads to a dispersion of the fire and is therefore to be avoided.

Before fire is opened, it should be borne in mind that the number of rounds in the men's possession is limited, and that the consumption of a certain amount of ammunition means an expenditure of force which should only be allowed in a situation where it will repay itself. On the other hand, the decision once made to fire at a certain object, the ammunition necessary to attain the object of the engagement must be employed to the full, as ineffective fire weakens the *morale* of one's own troops and strengthens that of the enemy's.

Sometimes the circumstances of the combat will admit, at the moment of opening fire, of the method of shooting in order to ascertain what sights should be used.

This method, however, is only applicable if the ground just in front of the object can be seen into, if the object itself is fixed and not hidden in powder-smoke, the conformation of the ground admits of the impact of the bullets being observed, one's own detachment is not under heavy fire, and, lastly, there is time enough for the trial shots to be made. As these conditions seldom exist together, the ability to get the correct sights by shooting is only exceptionally to be looked for. In shooting for the sights, volleys will be fired by half *züge* or *züge*, only one sight being used and one point of the object fired at. For the first volley, the sight is to be chosen so short that the points of impact of the bullets may be confidently expected to lie in front of the object. The proceeding will be continued as long as may be required and with sights gradually raised, until the proper sight is ascertained.

4. *Employment of different kinds of Fire.*

The rapidity of the fire is determined by the object of the fight, the formation of the object, and the ammunition available. Powder-smoke in front of the firing line, and unfavourable light, will frequently have a restraining effect on the rapidity of fire.

Against low objects at moderate distances, slow fire will generally be employed, if such objects are fired at at all. Rapid fire is indicated at short distances and against objects which are only visible for a short time at a favourable height for aiming. Against artillery, too, at distances beyond 800 metres, rapid fire will generally be appropriate.

As to the kinds of fire, volleys (*Salven*) and mass fire (*Schützenfeuer*)* are employed. Volleys can be fired when the

---

* *Schützenfeuer* may also be translated as "fire of skirmishers." The term "mass fire," adopted by Captain C. B. Mayne, in his work on "Infantry Fire Tactics" (chap. xiv), will, however, be employed in this translation. The term "individual fire (*or* firing)" has a special meaning attached to it (page 70).— (TRANSLATOR.)

rifle is used as a single loader or as a magazine loader, and therefore we distinguish them as *volleys* and *magazine volleys*. As regards mass fire we make a distinction, according to the rapidity of fire, between *slow* and *rapid mass fire* (when the rifle is used as a single-loader), and *magazine fire* (*Magazinfeuer* or *Schnellfeuer*) in which the rapidity of fire is increased to the utmost by the use of the magazine.

a. The Volley.—With volleys—volleys fired in line or swarm formation—the troops are most surely kept in hand, and the observation of the point of impact of the bullets, and consequently the selection of the sights to be used, facilitated.

As in the din of battle the voice will with difficulty be heard throughout a *zug* in close formation, and will seldom be plainly heard in the case of a *zug* in swarm formation, the employment of the volley is restricted to the commencement of the engagement and to moments when the troops are not actually under fire.

b. Mass Fire.—The fire of a firing line (*Schützenlinie*) will as a rule be delivered in the form of mass fire. This has the probability of producing the most effective result, owing to the men being able to aim calmly and wait for the most favourable moment for firing.

The firer must be so trained as to look for success, as a rule, not so much in rapid shooting as in well-aimed and deliberate fire. As regards habituation to firing slowly, each man must, as a rule, work in concert with the man next to him; while one of them fires the other watches, and the latter may (but need not necessarily) fire when the former has again loaded. If rapid fire is required, this alternate firing is discontinued. Each man fires as soon as he sees the object distinctly or finds a good opening in the powder-smoke in front of the enemy's line.

The greater or less rapidity of fire is either induced spontaneously or in response to the leader's call for "*rapid* (or *slow*) *fire.*" If the command for slackening the fire is not heard, the firing is stopped and so regulated.

If at the outset it is intended to open a slow or rapid fire, it is effected by the command "*Slow* (or *rapid*) *mass fire.*"

In addition to the distinction between rapid and slow mass fire, we distinguish between *controlled* fire, in which the influence of the leaders is still felt, and *uncontrolled* fire, when the firer must be left to act for himself.

c. Magazine Fire.—Magazine fire is intended to enhance the powers of the troops in decisive moments by reason of the motion of loading being suspended. It can be delivered either in open or close order, and also when necessary as magazine volleys.

If it is wished that the chief advantage of the magazine charge, increased readiness of fire, should be available at the decisive moment, no use should be made of the magazine fire at medium and long distances. At such distances the readiness

§ 39. CHOICE OF SIGHTS AND POINT TO BE AIMED AT.

Sights.

1. Up to 600 meters (656 yards), as a general principle, only one sight will be used.
2. Beyond 600 metres, as a rule, two sights differing by 100 metres (109·3 yards) will be used simultaneously. If the correct sighting is ascertained by observation, one elevation will at once be adopted.
3. Against objects advancing or retiring beyond 600 metres, as a rule, two sights differing by 100 metres will be used simultaneously.
4. Two sights will be employed by ranks; the front rank using the lower, the rear rank the higher elevation.

It is not advantageous to allow detachments under the strength of a zug to employ two sights.

Selection of Point of Aim.

Up to 400 metres, each man will select his point of aim in accordance with the directions given for target practice. Beyond 400 metres, as a rule, aim will be taken at the bottom of the object.

Any other point of aim can only be recommended (after due observation) when one sight alone is used.

§ 40. DIRECTION OF FIRE AND FIRE DISCIPLINE.

I. DIRECTION OF FIRE.

In General.

In action, as long as the direction of fire is to be maintained, the utilisation of the rifles must rest with the leaders. The rational direction of fire constitutes the real power of fire, and is therefore an essential guarantee of success.

Necessary conditions for exercising this direction are calm deliberation, tactical judgment, readiness in judging distance, good powers of observation, correct appreciation of the ground, and knowledge of the ballistic properties of the rifle; and these qualifications can only be acquired by the leaders through constant practice.

Speaking generally, the following duties appertain to the direction of fire :—

1. *Choice of Position on which to accept Musketry Combat and Rational Deployment of the Troops.*

Tactical considerations have the greatest weight in selecting the position to be occupied. Full utilisation of the power of fire is only possible on an open field of fire.

Apart from the actual size of the position chosen, the strength of the force to be deployed depends upon the object in view, the amount of ammunition that must necessarily be expended in order to obtain a certain result, and the time at disposal during which it can be employed.

In comparison with the probable result, and if the effect must be obtained within a short space of time, fire at distances beyond 800 metres (875 yards) requires the deployment of comparatively strong detachments.

The direction of fire is facilitated if definite sections can be indicated for the occupation of the several *züge* on their deployment, and distinctly defined intervals can be left between them, while the *züge* themselves are not broken up. Still, in order to diminish the losses resulting from the enemy's fire, it will in many cases be necessary for the individual *züge* to assume a less compact formation.

2. *Judging the Distance.*

If time and opportunity admit of it, the distances to specially well-defined points in the foreground, at which the enemy will probably appear, are to be ascertained by pacing or measurement, and notified to all. If such points do not exist, the distances 400, 600 and 800 metres will be determined in a similar manner and indicated by marks which are easily seen on our own side and cannot be mistaken, but which are not conspicuous on the enemy's side. Within 400 metres the distances can be ascertained by the groups themselves.

If time and opportunity fail, the distance can be ascertained by guessing, by questioning artillery or infantry who are firing in the immediate vicinity, or by examining good maps or using suitable portable measuring instruments. The reliability of the result obtained by guess is increased if the latter is not made by one individual only, but the average of the estimates made by several persons independently is taken.

The *zug* leader, therefore, keeps two or three good judges of distance near him, who on an object appearing in sight at once judge its distance and communicate their several estimates to the leader. These render the further assistance to the latter, that they keep in view not only the object to be fired at, but the other portions of the field of battle.

3. *Choice of Objective and Moment for Opening Fire. Determining the Sight to be Employed by Means of Firing.*

The selection of the object to be fired at is determined, first and foremost, by its tactical importance; after that, fire should be directed on such objects as, by reason of their height, depth, of fire of the single loader is sufficient. As a rule magazine fire is only used in combination with the standing sight or small flap.

Suitable occasions for the employment of magazine fire are as follows:—

a. In the attack: the last preparation before the final rush;

b. In the defence: the repulse of the enemy's final rush;

c. Repulse of cavalry, and all situations in which a sudden and immediate collision with the enemy occurs (fights in intrenchments, localities, woods, &c.);

d. Fire against a retreating adversary.

In the situations indicated above under *a*, *b*, and *d*, the control of fire will frequently be wholly or partially suspended, and employment of the magazine left entirely to the judgment of the individual man. The latter, therefore, in order that the most valuable property of the weapon may not be wasted at an unseasonable time, must be thoroughly trained to reserve the magazine for moments in which the immediate decision of the combat is sought, or imminent danger must be warded off.

Only exceptionally is magazine fire to be used at distances between 300 and 800 metres in cases in which the power of firing at particularly favourable objects is restricted to a brief period, and an increased fire effect at that moment is demanded by tactical considerations.

If the magazine is empty, the immediate refilling of it impossible, and the soldier or formed body compelled to deliver the most rapid fire possible, the rifle must be used as a single loader, the operations of loading and aiming being executed with the utmost celerity, so that the rapidity of fire may exceed that obtained in rapid mass firing.

5. *Giving Orders.*

The bringing the fire to bear upon the selected objects is one of the most difficult tasks of the direction of fire, and can only be effected by specific indication of the objects, and a uniform method of giving words of command. The command, which must be as short as possible, must, first of all, indicate the direction, then the object, the sight, and, lastly, the kind of fire required. The description of the object ought to be such as to exclude all possibility of misunderstanding; hostile detachments are to be spoken of as seen from our own side; thus, for example, "*the guns on the extreme right,*" and not "*the left flank of the battery.*"

Long words of command must be broken up into short sentences, and the leader will not begin a sentence until the preceding one has been repeated by the most distant group leaders. Excessive rapidity in giving words of command is to be carefully avoided, as a hasty, unaimed, and ineffective fire would be the result. Examples:—

" *On the green knoll—Artillery—Sights* 800 *and* 900*—Rapid mass fire;*" or,

" *Straight in front—Skirmishers lying down—Sight* 500*—Mass fire;*" or,

" *At the white house—Cavalry—Small flap—Magazine fire;*" or,

"*Magazine—Present—Fire—Load.*"

The firing in a volley must be even, *i.e.,* all the rifles must be fired together. To this end, the leader will modify the length of pause between "*present*" and "*fire*" according to the position of present adopted and the distance.

If the fire is to be stopped, the command " *Cease firing*" is given, or, if that cannot be distinguished, the whistle is sounded, repeated by all the group leaders. The whistle is a call to attention, and demands the immediate suspension of firing or loading motions, instant and unconditional quietude, and attention to the word of command.

If the fire is to be continued against the same object, the latter is not named again, and the command is simply "*Continue firing.*"

If only one of the sights in use has to be changed, and the other is to be retained, the command is given (*e.g.*) " *Change the* 800 *to* 1000," " *Continue Firing.*"

If the leader wishes to change the point of aim or the rapidity of fire, he gives the order (*e.g.*), using the whistle if necessary, "*Aim at the head*" (or "*below the object*"), or " *Slow (rapid) fire.*"

6. *Observation of the Effect of Fire.*

Continuous observation, with the help of good field-glasses, is necessary, in order to be able to judge from the dust raised by bullets, or from the enemy's behaviour, whether the sights and point of aim have been judiciously chosen, or what corrections are necessary to increase the fire effect.

With a view to being able to observe the effect of fire, leaders of the firing line, in choosing their own position, must bear in mind the direction of the wind. If immediate observation from the firing line itself is interfered with by the powder-smoke, it is advisable, if possible, to post special observers in trenches, &c., on one side, who will communicate their observations to the firing detachment by means of preconcerted signals, by calling out to them, or through intermediate posts.

7. *Duties of the several Ranks.*

The spheres of duty of the leaders of various rank, with regard to the direction of fire, although they cannot be sharply defined in some respects, are in general terms as follows:—

The battalion commander and the higher leaders indicate to

the troops the direction of the advance or the position to be taken up. They will indicate the objective in a general way, but will only exceptionally be in a position to order the opening of the fire. They will take steps for ensuring the supply of fresh ammunition in good time.

The company chief indicates the position to the *züge*, takes steps to ascertain the distances to important points in the foreground, orders, as a rule, the commencement of the fire, and as long as possible defines the objects to be fired at. He regulates the movements of the company, observes the enemy and the effect of the fire upon him, and looks after the replenishment of the ammunition with the means available on the battle-field, and the distribution to the *züge* of the ammunition brought up from the rear.

The *zug* leader superintends the occupation of the allotted position by the *zug*, and defines the object to be fired at according to the order of the company chief, or of his own initiative if the orders of the latter cannot be heard any longer in the further course of the fight. He orders the sights to be used, and the commencement and nature of the firing, directs from which pouch the cartridges are to be taken first, watches the effect of the fire, and stops it when required. He takes every means in his power, as long as the circumstances of the fight admit of it, to ensure an economical expenditure of ammunition proportionate to the object in view. He keeps his eye on the movements of the enemy, and uses every endeavour to act in concert with the neighbouring *züge* in the fighting line.

The group leader is responsible for the disposal of his group in the position assigned to it. As long as possible he watches over the adjustment of the sights, and the proper handling of the rifles, controls the expenditure of ammunition, and looks after the charging of the magazines. He observes the impact of the bullets, and repeats the orders of the *zug* leader when he observes that these are no longer understood in the neighbouring groups. He uses the whistle which forms part of his equipment whenever the *zug* leader's whistle sounds.

II. Fire Discipline.

Fire discipline includes the conscientious carrying out of orders during the musketry combat, and the rigid observance of the regulations regarding the handling of the rifle and conduct during the fight. It demands, further, calm endurance under the enemy's fire, even when this cannot yet be replied to, carefulness in firing, and utilisation of the ground so as to ensure the most effective result possible, constant attention both to the leaders and to the enemy, and ceasing to fire the moment the object disappears, the leader's whistle sounds, or in any other way the order to stop the firing is given.

Fire discipline must be so ingrained in the men that it will continue to influence them even when, in the course of the engagement, the direction of fire on the part of the leader can be but imperfectly exercised or ceases altogether, and when, at last, the behaviour of the firing line can only be determined by the individual reflection of each man, or the example of exceptionally daring and observant men. In order to develop and quicken the power of acting independently, the men must be accustomed to situations of the fight in which the direction of fire ceases altogether, and must be instructed as to their conduct in such circumstances. It must be laid down, in general, for the conduct of the musketry combat, when the proper leading fails, that under 400 metres all objects may be fired at, between 400 and 800 metres only high and wide objects can be (not must be) fired at, and that beyond 800 metres, as a rule, no more firing should take place.

§ 41. PREPARATORY EXERCISES.

For the preparatory exercises, blank or practice cartridges are used. The magazine is always to be loaded, even if with only a few cartridges, in order that the man may become accustomed to look upon it as a stand-by for special occasions.

As objectives, detachments are employed, which act according to bugle sounds or signals as previously arranged; artillery and cavalry can be represented by men with flags of a particular colour or by targets. The power of rapid observation and decision on the part of the leaders is exercised, and the readiness of the men to fire is quickened, by different objects appearing at unknown distances, and from having to calculate the time required to deploy the troops, and the period during which the object may be considered as visible or present.

Exercises by files are followed by others in groups. The men are instructed as to their behaviour in the attack and on the defensive, their skill in sighting, presenting and alternate fire is tested, and they are practised in rising rapidly to advance by rushes, and in skilfully and quickly occupying a fresh position after advancing. When the instruction by groups is completed, gradual exercises in half-*züge*, *züge*, and companies made up to war strength will follow. In the arrangement of the exercises the object to be kept in view is not only to train the leaders in their duties during the varying phases of the fight, but also to make the men act independently.

The *zug* and group leaders are accordingly to be made to fall out occasionally, so that the men may learn to act for themselves when the direction of fire fails. In criticising the decision and actions of individuals, the directing officer must bear in mind that the conduct of the men in the various phases of the fight ought not to be too much restricted by hard and fast rules; on the contrary, the self-reliance and decision of character of the officers and individual men must be constantly fostered.

These exercises will begin with the men of the youngest annual class after their incorporation in the company, and will thereafter be continued without break.

§ 42. EXERCISES WITH BALL CARTRIDGE.

The exercises with ball cartridge will be conducted in a similar manner to that prescribed in § 41; the objects are arrangements of targets, among which will be included, whenever possible, moving targets and such as appear and disappear suddenly. The appearance of such objects as are considered to be firing becomes much more like what it would be in real warfare, if some powder is fired in front of them, even if at their first appearance only. This is especially the case with regard to objects which appear at great distances (as, for example, artillery), and whose appearance might otherwise be easily overlooked, or not observed until after some time.

Simple tactical suppositions are to underlie these exercises, regard being had not merely to the conditions of field operations, but also to those of fortress warfare. As to the mode of procedure in the latter case, the indications given under the head of "instructional firing" will apply.

During the pauses necessary for criticising the operations, the results of the firing must be ascertained, and compared with the expenditure of ammunition. These results are not entered in the musketry returns, but in the musketry sheets the days will be noted on which each man has taken part in the field firing exercises of a formed body. If superior officers wish to be informed of the course of individual exercises, the reports rendered will be in the briefest form, and not encumbered with complicated figures.

The extent of the exercises will be more particularly regulated by the number of cartridges allotted to the troops by the army corps commander as a supplementary issue from the ammunition at his disposal. In apportioning this supplementary allowance, it is advisable, instead of making an equal distribution all round, to enable the troops in turn to carry out an exercise on a large scale in addition to the minor exercises. If local circumstances do not admit of extensive operations being carried out against objects in connection with fortress warfare, the conditions which have to be considered in such exercises will be demonstrated in the course of instructional firing.

Owing to the conditions which obtain in peace, the several stages of the fighting exercises succeed each other very much quicker than they would do in reality, and accordingly the troops nearly always fire much more rapidly at these exercises than the situation and number of rounds carried by the men would admit of in real warfare. In order that this peace habit may not have a detrimental effect on active service, both leaders and men are to be thoroughly instructed on this point.

In field firing the leaders must occupy the same position,

and assume the same attitude as they would have to do in the
actual fight. It is only by frequent practice in this way that
they can overcome the very much greater difficulties, as compared with the standing position, which are presented by the
kneeling and lying down positions in controlling one's own men
and observing the enemy.

The exercises are to begin with the men of the youngest
annual class in the last quarter of their first year of service,
and in the case of other men to be practised at all times of the
year. For the purpose of forming detachments of war strength,
men of different companies may be combined together.

It must be borne in mind that the advantages to be gained
from these exercises are determined by the manner in which
they are conducted, and that progress can only be secured by
uninterrupted practice.

VIII. INSTRUCTIONAL FIRING.

§ 43. IN GENERAL.

Instructional firing is intended to demonstrate the ballistic
properties of the rifle and the conditions under which the
fullest advantage can be taken of them, and so to illustrate
practically the fundamental principles for the employment of
the weapon. It not only forms an excellent auxiliary means
for forming a well-trained and expert instructional staff, but is
also well fitted to instruct the men as to their conduct in battle
when the direction of fire fails.

The more elementary exercises in instructional firing are to
be exhibited to the under-officers and men by the company-
chief as near the beginning of the firing exercises as possible;
in the case of more important exercises, it is advisable that the
battalion commanders should direct the exercises.

In arranging the exercises, care is to be taken that all influences which might prejudice the result are as far as possible
excluded.

On this account the exercises, are carried out as a rule at
known distances, in favourable weather, and, so far as applicable, with rifles on rests.

The directions for ensuring the security of the adjoining
ground and of the markers, laid down for field firing, are applicable in their entirety to instructional firing.

In the following observations only the most important instructional firing exercises are specified.

§ 44. DEMONSTRATION OF THE BALLISTIC PROPERTIES OF THE RIFLE.

The order of dress is the same as that prescribed for the
preliminary exercises.

(3269)   E

1. *Ascertaining the Situation of the Points of Impact of Different Rifles.*

A good shot sitting behind a table with rifles on the rest, fires 5 shots at the same target at 100 metres from each of 3 rifles, without altering the sights and point of aim; one rifle being an accurate shooter, one shooting too high, and the third too short.

The mean point of impact of the 5 shots fired from one rifle gives the situation of the point of impact for that weapon.

The comparison of the situations of the point of impact thus ascertained for these arms teaches that one single point of aim cannot be fixed upon which will suit all rifles, and that consequently the soldier, especially if he wishes to hit a small object, must take into consideration the peculiarities of his own rifle when selecting the point at which he will aim.

2. *Demonstration of Accuracy of Shooting at Distances of* 200, 250, 350, 450, *and* 600 *metres.*

A good shot, sitting behind a table with rifle on the rest, fires 25 shots at each of the distances 200, 250, 350, and 450 metres, at a section target placed on edge, and at 600 metres at a screen 133·8 inches high formed of 2 section targets. Marks are placed on the target to show the point aimed at.

A comparison of the extent of the shot-groupings with the various objects that would be met with in the field illustrates the reason for fixing the limits, imposed by the degree of accuracy of the weapon itself, within which there is a probability of each shot hitting.

3. *Illustration of the Path described by a Bullet, by showing the heights of Trajectory when the Standing Sight, small Flap, and 400-metre Sight are used.*

A good shot, sitting behind a table, with rifle (a normal shooting weapon) on the rest, fires 5 shots under each of the following conditions:—

(*a.*) With the standing sight and (*b*) with the small flap at distances of 50, 100, 150, and 200 metres;

(*c.*) With the small flap only at 250 and 300 metres;

(*d.*) With the 400-metre sight at 100, 200, 300, 350, and 400 metres.

The point aimed at is the bottom of the target or mark at its lower edge.

A section target placed on edge is sufficient for each distance.

The position of the mean shot at each distance gives the height of the mean trajectory above the line of sight for that distance; and with good shooting this will approximately agree with the measurements of the trajectories given in § 7, 3.

After distinguishing the mean point of impact on each target by a bright-coloured plaster, visible from afar and of a distinct colour for each sight, the targets are placed one behind the other at the corresponding distances. In this way a clear picture of the trajectories and their heights at the several distances is obtained.

If a man stands, kneels, or lies down, close to each target, the position of the points of impact on the human body is seen, and a lesson imparted as to the choice of sights and points to aim at.

4. *Demonstration of the Effect of Fixing the Bayonet.*

A man fires 5 shots at 200 metres without the bayonet, and 5 shots with bayonet fixed, aiming at the same point in both cases.

A comparison of the position of the mean points of impact shows the deviation of the bullet, to the left and downwards, caused by fixing the bayonet.

§ 45. FIRING UNDER SPECIAL CIRCUMSTANCES.

For the order of dress, see § 34, 3, second sentence.

1. *Shooting from Shelter Trenches by Day under Conditions of Siege Warfare.*

(*a.*) Single men fire at 200 metres from behind cover at targets which are also placed behind cover (embrasures, screens, sand-bags). The opening in the enemy's cover, through which the bullet must enter in order to hit, is to be about 3·9 inches high and 1·9 inches wide.

It is sufficient if targets of the size and colour of the supposed cover are used as objects, the embrasures being represented by a darker colour.

The men in the vicinity of those firing observe the shots and state the results of their observations.

This exercise gives an opportunity of learning the sorts of cover which are used in siege warfare, and the influence they have upon the shooting; it also teaches the importance of accurate observation and corresponding correction of fire when the object is small.

(*b.*) Detachments of greater or less strength fire from shelter trenches at distances of 400 and 600 metres (say 440 and 660 yards), or, when longer ranges are available or the firing is conducted in the open, at 400 and 700 metres (770 yards), at broad and low targets, 13·7 inches high, which when the firing is in the open are placed on a parapet or mound.

E 2

At 400 metres also disappearing targets of the same size are fired at.

Although the distance is known, endeavour will always be made at the very first to test the correctness of the sights adopted, or of the point aimed at, by means of volleys. It is to be noticed that in siege warfare, as a rule, the hits observed in front of the object afford the only means of correcting the sights and point aimed at.

Instructional firing illustrates the fire effect which is to be expected at different distances in firing from shelter trenches at the objects to be met with in siege warfare, and teaches how it may be heightened by means of careful observation and suitable corrections.

2. *Shooting from Shelter Trenches by Night with the help of Rests.*

Detachments of greater or less strength fire at night from shelter trenches at distances of 200 to 700 metres against targets which represent large bodies of troops, using rests which are adapted to keep the rifle in a given position and direction.

During the day, the men are instructed in arranging the rifles as they lie on the rests and also in fixing the latter. It is also advisable to let them fire by day in the same way as they will have to do at night, so that it can be ascertained at the conclusion of the firing, whether the rests still retain approximately the position originally given them. The men will in this way more easily recognize and learn to avoid the mistakes they have made in using the rest, than they could do if they only fired by night. For night firing, the rests are not placed on the parapets and the rifles arranged on them until twilight has set in. The firing itself is not begun until it is perfectly dark.

The object of this exercise is to make officers, non-commissioned officers, and men, familiar with the use of the rests which are used in siege warfare for night firing or during a fog, and with the handling of the rifles placed on them, and also to prove to them that if night firing is conducted in a proper manner comparatively favourable results may be attained.

IX. MUSKETRY INSPECTION.

The musketry inspection (*Prüfungsschiessen*) is divided into individual musketry inspection on the ranges and musketry inspection in the open field. The former is calculated to furnish as uniform a basis as possible on which to found a judgment as to the skill of the troops in target practice, while the latter gives the superior officers an opportunity to satisfy themselves as to the training in field firing, under conditions which approximate as nearly as possible to those which obtain in real warfare.

§ 46. INDIVIDUAL MUSKETRY INSPECTION.

The exercise is to be carried out on the ranges in July or August, if possible in fine weather, in the way prescribed in the following form; it will be performed under the direction of the regimental-commander, or, in the case of isolated battalions, under that of the battalion-commander.

Before the firing commences the directing officer satisfies himself as to the correctness of the target measurements. Officers are charged with the supervision of the markers and the recording of the results. The hits are to be given in whole numbers; in calculating the percentages, fractions of $\frac{1}{2}$ and over are to be reckoned as 1, fractions under $\frac{1}{2}$ are not counted.

At the end of the report a statement regarding the weather, temperature, light and wind is to be added.

The report, drawn up in accordance with the following form, will be submitted with the musketry report.

REPORT

On the Individual Musketry Inspection of the —— Battalion,
—— Regiment.

I. Individual firing of the men on the (date).

A. *General Remarks.*

(1.) 60 men per company (or 72 in battalions on the higher establishment) take part in this exercise.

(2.) Order of dress as for the principal exercises in target practice; the packing (or weighting) of the knapsack is not done until the men reach the ranges.

(3.) Each man fires 5 rounds in the same way as at target practice.

B. *Exercises.*

(1.) The 20 (or 24) men of the last annual class but one (men in their 2nd year of service), whom the company-chief considers to be the best shots of the class, fire at 200 metres, standing, with hands free, at a ring target.

Hits made by	Total.			Per cent.		
	Hits.	Men's breadths, including bullseyes.	Bulls-eyes.	Hits.	Man's breadths, including bullseyes.	Bulls-eyes.
Company, with rounds....						
" " "						
" " "						
" " "						
Total men with rounds						

(2.) The 20 (or 24) men of the youngest annual class, whom the company-chief considers to be the best shots of the class, fire at 200 metres, standing, with hands free, at a ring target.

(Here follows the same Form as above.)

(3.) The 20 (or 24) men of the youngest annual class, whom the company-chief considers to be the next best shots of the class, fire at 200 metres, standing, with rest, at a ring target.

If it is not possible to fill up this second detachment of men of the youngest class, it must be made up with men in the 3rd shooting class who belong to the oldest two annual classes and who are shown by the Musketry Book to be the worst shots. The regimental (or battalion) commanders will satisfy themselves that recourse is not had to this alternative without sufficient grounds, which will be explained at the end of the report.

(Here follows the same Form as above.)

II. Individual firing of the under-officers on the (date).

    A. General remarks (1, 2, and 3, as above).
    B. Exercise.

6 under-officers of each company, chosen by the company-chief, fire at 200 metres, standing, with hands free, at a ring target.

(Here follows the same Form as above.)

Remarks :—

Name and rank of directing officer.

§ 47. MUSKETRY INSPECTION IN THE OPEN FIELD.

The musketry inspection in the open field will be held annually in each battalion by the brigade commander, unless the divisional or army corps commander prefers personally to direct the exercises, which must always be recognized as inspections. The exercises, the arrangement of which is settled by the superior officers who direct them to be held, will give a just view of the efficiency of a battalion and enable a definite judgment to be formed of the intelligence of the leaders and the training of the men in field firing, especially if the detachments are made up to war strength and the exercises are combined with a march under service conditions.

If it is impracticable to hold the musketry inspection in the field in any year, the ammunition allotted for the purpose (*i.e.*, the balance of the ammunition provided for musketry inspection, after deducting the number of rounds used for individual musketry inspection) will either be utilized for other exercises in field firing, or will be retained for similar purposes in the following year. If the number of rounds allotted for any particular exercise in the field is not wholly expended at that exercise, the surplus is to be used for special exercises for the officers, and it is forbidden to apply it to any other purpose.

Special reports on the musketry inspection in the field will not be appended to the musketry reports.

X. FIRING WITH THE REVOLVER.

§ 48. APPARATUS AND ARRANGEMENTS FOR REVOLVER FIRING.

1. The targets used are the figure target and its modifications.

2. The same rest is used as for firing with the rifle.

3. Revolver table. This is a rectangular table, the top of which is arranged as a stand on which 6 or 8 revolvers can be placed, and also for holding the packets of cartridges and cleaning apparatus.

A. COURSE OF TRAINING.

§ 49. IN GENERAL.

The following ranks are to be trained in the use of the revolver:—Officers, vice-serjeant-majors, colour bearers, regimental and battalion drummers, and such under-officers and men as are exercised as sick-bearers, or who are intended to be employed with sanitary detachments.

The training with the revolver must be of such a nature as to ensure a rational use of the weapon in battle.

The exercises must be preceded by thorough instruction in the construction of the revolver and in the combined action of the several parts, as, owing to the shortness of the weapon, incautious or incorrect handling makes it much more dangerous to the firer and those near him than is the case with the rifle. Moreover, unskilful handling is liable to cause injury to the several parts of the revolver and to affect its durability.

The preliminary exercises begin with aiming, after which follow loading, cocking, securing, and releasing, and instruction in presenting and pulling off.

The last stage of the preliminary exercises consists of firing blank cartridge. In doing this, the firing rest will be used at first, the firer at the same time aiming at a target.

§ 50. AIMING.

Bearing in mind that the operation of aiming has already been learnt during rifle instruction, the exercises in aiming should be chiefly directed to familiarising the firer with the comparatively shorter length of the line of sight.

At first a firing rest will be used.

§ 51. LOADING, COCKING, SECURING, RELEASING, AND UNLOADING.

In the first place it must be impressed upon the firer that the revolver must always be held with the muzzle outwards, and in such a way that the axis of the barrel produced shall point slightly in front of the toes. Only in presenting will the muzzle be moved from this position and directed towards the object.

1. *Loading and Cocking.*—The soldier receives the revolver at the revolver table, moves up to the firing point, takes the weapon in his left hand, and with the thumb of the right hand places the hammer at half-cock. To do this, the entire right-hand grasps the butt, while the thumb, covering the comb from right to left, draws back the hammer with the root of the first joint until a click is heard.

After opening the loading flap, the cylinder is turned round to the right with the thumb and middle finger of the left hand, and after each sixth of a revolution a cartridge is pushed into the cartridge chamber so far that its base is flush with the hinder surface of the cylinder. The firer names the number of the cartridge each time he inserts one into a chamber.

After loading the number of cartridges provided, the loading flap is closed. In order to cock the revolver, the thumb of the right hand draws the hammer back, as in half-cocking, until a second click is perceived. In order to avoid unintentional discharge of the weapon and injuries to the half-bent, a hammer which has been drawn back should not be let go until it has been brought to full-cock.

The forefinger of the right hand is next placed within the trigger-guard, the finger-nail on the left border of the inner surface of the guard. The remaining fingers of the right hand grasp the small of the stock firmly and uniformly. The left hand, which until now has supported the revolver under the cylinder, moves to the left hip.

2. *Securing and Releasing.*—The revolver can only be directly secured when the hammer is down or in half-cock position. It is secured by the right hand grasping the butt while the thumb of the left hand presses the safety-catch downwards.

If the weapon is to be secured when at the full-cock, the hammer is first drawn slightly backward, and then, while the forefinger presses the trigger, lowered slowly on to the plate, the thumb holding it firmly, and the left hand meanwhile supporting the revolver at the cylinder. The hammer is then brought back to the half-cock, and the thumb of the left hand presses the safety-catch downwards.

If it is wished to release the catch, the right hand grasps the revolver at the butt, while the thumb of the left hand presses the safety-catch forwards. Thus, if the right is otherwise occupied and the left merely supporting the revolver, the motions of securing and releasing are usually performed by the left hand, but they can also be executed by the thumb of the right hand if the left is not free (owing to holding the sword or reins).

3. *Unloading.*—If a revolver is to be unloaded, or if the cases are to be removed after the cartridges have been fired,

the hammer will be brought to the half-cock and secured, and the weapon handed over to the under-officer at the revolver-table, with the report "It is loaded" or "It has been fired." The under-officer takes the revolver in his left hand, holds it over the table and opens the loading-flap. He then inserts the unloading-rod, or a stick about 8 inches long and $\frac{1}{8}$ inch thick, into the front opening of the chambers and removes the cartridges or cases from the cylinder, turning the latter gradually with the left hand towards the right.

§ 52. PRESENTING AND FIRING.

The body must be held firmly but without constraint. Particular care must be taken that the right arm is not stiff at the elbow and wrist, and that the forefinger does not come into play too soon when the firer presents.

At first the revolver is used on the rest, but subsequently the present will be practised with hand free.

1. *Presenting, using the rest.* The firer places himself facing the target, grasps the butt with the right hand, and takes his proper distance from the firing rest, placing the muzzle of the revolver with extended right arm on the rest. The weapon is then loaded and cocked without being secured. The left hand being placed on the hip, the firer turns half-left and places the right foot about half a pace to the right on the new front. In other respects the instructions for the position of the body when firing with the rifle are to be followed, so far as applicable.

The eyes being directed towards the object, the right hand raises the revolver, the muzzle of which is slightly directed upwards, until the fore-sight is on a level with the eye. The right arm, slightly bent and with unstiffened wrist, is then extended towards the point of aim and the revolver gently lowered on to the rest. The line of sight, which will already have been recognized by the eye, is directed on the point of aim, and at the same time the forefinger of the right hand feels the tongue of the trigger.

Slight differences in height are to be compensated for by stepping sideways, forwards or backwards.

It is important that the right hand should always grasp the butt at the same place, and not sometimes lower and another time higher.

2. *Firing.*—Firing is effected by the forefinger getting a firm feeling of the tongue of the trigger at the time the line of aim is taken, and that as far as possible with the root of the first joint, and drawing the trigger back with a gradually increasing pressure until the hammer frees itself from the top-bent and suddenly discharges the cartridge. In doing this no part of the body should move except the forefinger, and the revolver must be directed as fixedly as possibly towards the object at the moment of pulling off.

3. *Presenting with hand free.*—This is not practised until the firer has acquired some skill in presenting and firing by means of using the rest.

B. Firing Exercises.

§ 53. In General.

The firing exercises with the revolver are held by companies in the same way as in the case of exercises with the rifle.

The company chief decides as to the disposal of surplus cartridges.

Dress: forage caps and side arms.

§ 54. Duty with the Firing Detachment and at the Target.

1. The duties of the superintending staff are the same as those prescribed in the case of firing with the rifle, so far as they are not modified by the following directions.

The superintending *personnel* consists of the following :—

a. The officer, who is under no circumstances whatever to be replaced by a sword-knot under-officer. He takes post on the right side of the firer.

b. The under-officer for superintending the firer, who stands on his right and slightly in rear of him, and gives him the cartridges to be loaded one by one from a cartridge packet.

c. The under-officer for looking after the arms and ammunition. His post is at the revolver table, which is placed a few paces behind the firing detachment. He gives each man the arm intended for him just before it is his turn to fire, serves out the cartridges in packages as required to the under-officer mentioned above, and removes all unfired cartridges and empty cases from the revolvers, which are given up to him as soon as the firing is finished.

d. The writer.

2. The firing detachment, which should not exceed five men if it can be avoided, takes post a few paces in rear of the firing point facing the target. The man whose turn it is to fire goes to the revolver table to receive his weapon, and then moves up to the firing point. Here follow, as soon as firing is permissible in accordance with the rules laid down for firing with the rifle, the operations of loading the cartridges, which are given the man by the under-officer superintending him, and then those of cocking, presenting, and firing. As soon as a shot is fired, the man names the point actually aimed at and the number of his shot, removes his forefinger from inside the trigger-guard, withdraws the revolver, resuming his proper front by drawing back the right foot and dropping the left arm, and secures it without half-cocking. As soon as the marking is

finished, the revolver is released and cocked, and the same operation is repeated as in the previous shot.

If several shots follow each other without intermission, the forefinger remains within the trigger-guard. Cocking is then done entirely with the right hand, and either in the position of presenting or, if that is not practicable, by withdrawing the revolver quickly from that position towards the upper part of the thigh, and pressing the butt firmly against it during the motion of cocking. After cocking, the revolver is at once returned to the present.

If a firer is unsteady while presenting, he must withdraw his revolver, and secure it; if, owing to excitement, he is temporarily unable to proceed with the firing, the revolver, secured, must be given up at the revolver-table.

If a cartridge misses fire, it must be tried again from the same revolver, or if necessary once more from another weapon. If it still misses fire, it will be marked as a " total miss-fire."

The marking *personnel* acts in the same way as during firing with the rifle.

§ 55. MEASURES OF SECURITY.

For the purpose of preventing accidents, the same steps are to be taken as prescribed for shooting with the rifle, so far as the directions are not amplified or modified by the following rules :—

1. Before each firing practice, preparatory exercises with exercise or blank cartridges will be conducted elsewhere than at the ranges, at which the men will be instructed afresh in the handling and mechanism of the weapon.

2. Before each firing practice, the revolvers are to be examined in order to see that the hammer stands firmly at half-cock and that the cylinder is fixed when at full-cock, and also that the barrels and cylinders are free from foreign bodies.

When the exercise is over, the revolvers will be examined in order to see that cartridges and cases are removed, and a report to this effect will be made to the officer in charge.

3. While in firing with the rifle each man of the detachment which is formed up for firing carries his weapon, and has the number of rounds required for the exercise in his ammunition pouch, in shooting with the revolver only that man receives his weapon who is to move up to the firing point. The cartridges are handed to the firer singly, and at once inserted by him in the chambers.

Further, the man fires the whole of the rounds provided for the practice, whether the marking is done after each shot or after all the shots have been fired, and not until he has done so does he return to the detachment.

Revolvers, while not in use, are placed on the revolver table with the hammers down to the fullest extent, their muzzles directed away from the firing range; on the table, also, is all the ammunition which is not in the hands of the under-officer superintending the firer.

5. Loaded revolvers are invariably to be handed to second persons secured, and with the report "It is loaded;" similarly revolvers that have been fired will be half-cocked and secured, and only when that has been done will they be given up to the under-officer at the revolver table with the words, "It has been fired."

In unloading revolvers, and in extracting cases from them, they are to be held with the muzzles directed away from the firing range.

§ 56. Exercises.

No.	Metres.	Number of rounds and mode of conducting exercise.	Method of presenting.	Target.	Point aimed at.	Remarks.
1	20	5 consecutive shots, marking each shot.	With rest.	Figure.	Knee.	The accuracy of the weapon is such that a reliable shot will put every bullet into the figure target.
2	20	Ditto.	Hand free.	Ditto.	Ditto.	

Instead of the exercises shown above, the company-chief can order special ones for officers and under-officers who have shown great skill.

The exercises are entered in the sheet used for shooting with the rifle (no report). The expenditure of ammunition is shown in the form (No. 4) given in § 59.

§ 57. Trial Shots.

In cases in which bad shooting is ascribed to the faulty construction of a revolver, the officer directing the exercises is at liberty to fire, or cause to be fired, a few shots—termed trial shots—for the purpose of proving the weapon. These will be entered as a total in the rough musketry practice sheet and ammunition return.

XI. MUSKETRY BOOKS, REPORTS AND FORMS.

§ 58. Musketry Books.

1. The Company Musketry Book, full folio size, begins with a nominal roll of (1) officers, (2) under-officers, and (3) privates belonging to the company, numbered and arranged alphabetically in each class.

Next follows a summary of the firing days and ammunition expended, Form 1.

After this comes a list of the rifles numbered consecutively, with the names of the owners, and reference to the page of the musketry book on which the musketry sheet of each man is to be found.

This is followed by the musketry sheets (Form 2) numbered to correspond to the nominal roll at the beginning of the book.

At the end of the book is a duplicate of the report on the individual musketry inspection, and of the musketry report of the company.

The following signs are used for denoting the shots :—

(a.) For all targets.

0 = misses.

∞ = grazes which have hit the target.

(b.) For the band target.

$$\left.\begin{array}{c} 12 \\ 10\ 11 \\ \top\ \top \end{array}\right\} = \text{band in bullseye.}$$

| = band outside bullseye.

11,10 = bullseye outside band.

M = hit within man's breadth, but outside band.

+ = hit (target) outside man's breadth.

(c.) For the ring target.

1—12 = number of ring. A number crossed through denotes outside the man's breadth.

M = hit inside man's breadth, but outside ring.

+ = hit (target) outside man's breadth and ring.

(d.) For the figure target and its modifications.

F = figure.

(e.) For section target.

+ = hit.

The seat of the shot is to be marked as accurately as possible by a dot, e.g., in firing at the band target, by

$$\mid .M, \ M., \ \cdot + \ +.$$

in firing at the ring target, by

$$\overset{.}{9}, \ \cdot 9, \ \emptyset. \ \cdot \not{\emptyset}$$

All shots fired on the same day to complete an exercise will, as a rule, be shown on one line, and the number of shots will be given in the corresponding column. The five (or three) shots with which the condition is fulfilled will be underlined.

The company musketry books will be renewed annually, and the number of sheets is to be verified by the company-chiefs.

The companies use rough musketry practice sheets on the ranges, from which the shots are to be transferred to the company musketry book, which is always to be kept up to date.

An examination of the musketry books will enable the higher commanders to follow the course of training, or the system pursued by the companies in carrying out the exercises. It is forbidden to make extracts from the musketry books with the object of forming an opinion as to the efficiency of a company in musketry, based on the number of rounds fired and the hits made. Comparative estimates may be formed in the first place from the results of the special exercises and of the individual musketry inspection, and a further criterion is afforded by the number of men who have fulfilled all the conditions.

It is forbidden to issue special directions as to the mode of keeping the musketry books and musketry practice sheets; only the company-chief is authorized to settle the details within the scope of these Regulations.

2. The man's Musketry Small-book contains in portable form—

(a.) The description of the rifle;
(b.) The musketry sheet, as in the company musketry book,
(c.) Certificates of promotion from one class to another, musketry prizes, and shooting badges;
(d.) Description of shots;
(e.) Rules as to choice of sights and points to be aimed at for target practice, with aiming table (§ 28) and § 35 (Fire effect of individual shots). It is also recommended to enter in the musketry small-book the ascertained deviation of the man's rifle for each distance.

The musketry small-book remains in the possession of the man. It is given up to the writer at the firing range in order that the shots may be entered, and is returned into the man's hands before the detachment marches back from the range.

§ 59. MUSKETRY REPORTS.

1. The companies furnish the battalion, on the 1st November of each year, with the Musketry Report and Return of Ammunition, Forms 3 and 4.

2. The battalions compile a General Return from the company returns of ammunition. This return and the Battalion Musketry Report, Form 5, are forwarded to the regiment, together with the company returns.

3. The regiments submit the battalion reports and returns of ammunition, together with the Reports on the Individual Musketry Inspections to the higher authorities. The company musketry reports with enclosures are retained by the regiments, unless specially required by the higher authorities to be submitted to them.

4. The Army Corps Commanders submit the following

returns to His Majesty the Emperor and King by the 30th November of each year :—

(*a*.) The battalion musketry reports ; and

(*b*.) The reports on the individual musketry inspection ;

both series are in original, and bound in separate volumes.

The musketry reports of Landwehr Districts are not submitted.

Form 1.

SUMMARY OF FIRING DAYS AND AMMUNITION EXPENDED.

1	2 Firing days.			3	4 Took part in the exercises.											5 Ammunition expended.												6	7	8
					Special.		Shooting class. Ist			IInd			IIIrd				Special exercises.				Field firing.		Musketry inspection.					
Current number.	Day.	Month.	Year.	Nature of exercise.	Officers.	Under-officers.	Officers.	Under-officers.	Men.	Officers.	Under-officers.	Men.	Officers.	Under-officers.	Men.	Target practice.	Officers.	Under-officers and men.	Prize firing.	Trial shots.	Individual.	Detachment.	Individual.	In open field.	Instructional firing.	Total.	Complete miss-fires.	Unserviceable cartridges.	Remarks.
				E.g., target practice and special exercises.																									

(3269)   F

Musketry Sheet, No. .

1st Shooting Class.

Form 2.

Private ———.

Rifle No. .

1	2	3	4	5	6
No.	Description of exercise.	Date of exercise.	Succession and description of shots.	No. of shots.	Remarks.

Preliminary Practice.

1	100 metres, standing, with rest. Band target, 3 bullseyes with 2 bands, or 3 bands with 2 bullseyes.				
2	150 metres, standing, with rest. Ring target, 3 man'sbreadths, 2 bullseyes, 27 rings.				
3	150 metres, standing, hands free. Ring target, 3 man'sbreadths, 1 bullseye, 21 rings.				
			Total of preliminary practice.		Here will be inserted all necessary explanations regarding the course of training and exceptional circumstances, *e.g.*, leaving the service, employment on command, transfer, long-continued leave or sickness. Reasons for any lengthened break in a man's shooting practices, or for exercises succeeding each other too rapidly; grounds for not firing 3 (or 5) rounds on any practice day; remarks as to special peculiarities of rifle, trial shots, proving the rifle, cracked cartridge cases, unserviceable cartridges, complete miss-fires, &c.

Principal Practice.

4	150 metres, lying down, with rest. Head target, 3 figures.				
5	200 metres, standing, with rest, behind parapet. Disappearing breast target, 2 figures.				
6	300 metres, lying down, hands free. Double knee target, 3 figures.				
7	350 metres, kneeling. Double figure target, 3 figures.				
8	600 metres, kneeling. Section targets, 3 hits.				
9	200 metres, standing, hands free. Ring target, 5 hits, 4 man'sbreadths, 25 rings.				
10	150 metres, lying down, hands free. 4 trunk targets, no conditions —sufficient skill: 3 figures, 1 hit each.				
			Total of principal practice.		

1	2	3	4	5	6
No.	Description of exercise.	Date of exercise.	Succession and description of shots.	No. of shots.	Remarks.

Special Exercises (§ 14).

1					
2					
3					

Total expenditure of ammunition.

1. Fired at field firing, individual firing: (date).
2. Took part in field firing by formed bodies : (date).
3. Promotion into higher shooting class :
4. Musketry prizes and shooting badges :

NOTE.—The above form, with the necessary modifications, is also used for other shooting classes. It takes up two pages of the company musketry book.

In making out the report, Form 3, the following points will be attended to :—

1. The training of one year volunteers, and of those who are incorporated in April, will, as a rule, extend over the whole of their year of service. They will be included in the report of the year during which they are dismissed.

2. Men on leave "at disposal," who may be called in to complete the strength of the company after the 31st May, again take part in field firing, whenever possible, and fire twenty-five rounds at target practice under the orders of the company-chief. Those who are called in before the above-named date fire throughout the whole exercise of their shooting class.

3. Men who return from command, out of hospital, from fortress imprisonment, &c., and had not already begun the musketry exercises of the current musketry year, will be held to perform firing practices in the same way as laid down above for men on leave.

4. Men about the performance of whose service there is any uncertainty, who are incorporated on the 1st April or later, do not commence the musketry exercises until the next musketry year.

5. Officers, officer aspirants, and men on leave, who are only called in for purposes of exercise, and candidates for scholastic appointments, &c., are not shown in the musketry report.

Musketry Report.   Form 3.

Company.	Officers.	Under-officers.	Men.	Special. Officers.	Special. Under-officers.	Special. Men.	1st. Officers.	1st. Under-officers.	1st. Men.	2nd. Officers.	2nd. Under-officers.	2nd. Men.	3rd. Officers.	3rd. Under-officers.	3rd. Men.
									Of whom in the — Shooting class.						
1. Strength at end of last calendar year.															
2. Decrease — Have not begun the exercises. — *a.* On command.															
Have prematurely discontinued the exercises owing to having left. — *a.* On command.															
b. Discharged.															
Have completed a curtailed course on account of being — *a.* Men on leave at disposal called in after 31st May.															
Total ...															
3. Increase... — *a.* Transferred.															
b. Put back.															
Total ...															
4. Consequently had to complete all the target practice exercises (Nos. 1 + 3 − 2).															
5. Of the numbers given in (4). — *a.* Have not completed all the target practice exercises.															
b. Have completed all the target practice exercises, but not fulfilled all the conditions.															
c. Have completed all the target practice exercises for which conditions are prescribed.															
6. Of these there have been promoted into a higher class ..															

I. *Explanations [of preceding Report].*

Under 1. Including — one-year volunteers incorporated on
1st April, 18 , and — on 1st October, 18 .
&c.

Under 2. Decrease.

Not begun:
1. Sergeant X employed as writer in —————
since 1st October, 18 .
2.   &c.

Prematurely discontinued:
1. Sergeant X. appointed on 1st April, 18 , as
writer in—————
2.   &c.

Completed curtailed course:
1. Private X called in on 15th June, 18   , as man
on leave at disposal.
2.   &c.

Under 3. Increase :
1. Private X transferred from the — to this company.
2. Private X called in on 15th June, 18   , as man
on leave at disposal.
&c.

Under 5. Have not completed all exercises:
1. Private X on sick leave from 1st May to 15th
September, 18 .
2. Sergeant X on leave (or on command) from
20th May to 1st October, 18 .

II. *Gained Musketry Prizes.*

1. Under-officer: sergeant —————, — shooting
class.
2. Private —————, — shooting class.
&c.

III. *Obtained Shooting Badges.*

1. Under-officer: sergeant —————, — shooting
class.
2. Private ·—————, — shooting class.
&c.

IV. *Individual Musketry Inspection was held at* —————.

The following did not take part, or fired less than 15 rounds
(with statement of reasons) :—

(*Continued on page* 87.)

Form 4.

—— Company.

Return of Ammunition.

I. *For Rifles.*

1. For the musketry year 18— there were received..	2. — Staff Officers, each —.	3. — Captains and subalterns, each —.	4. — under-officers and privates, each —.	5. For musketry inspection.	6. For cartridge cases returned, &c. Surplus.	7. For Officers, &c., of the category "on leave;" candidates for scholastic appointments.	8. For special purposes.	9. Total.
			On account of officers, under-officers, and men with the colours.					
Expenditure shown.			On account of officers, under-officers and men of the "on leave" category; scholastic candidates, &c.					
Surplus							Total	

NOTE.—The ammunition for the incorporated one-year volunteers is to be accounted for in the year in which they complete their service.

1. *Explanations.*

1. Occasion on which fired.		2. Number of rounds fired.		3. Complete miss-fires.	4. Unserviceable cartridges.	5. Total.
		By officers, under-officers and men with the colours.	By officers, &c., of the "on leave" category, scholastic candidates, &c.			
a. Target practice.						
b. Special exercises.	Officers.					
	Under-officers and men.					
c. Prize firing.						
d. Trial shots.						
e. Field firing.	Individual.					
	In formed bodies.					
f. Musketry inspection.	Individual.					
	In open field.					
g. Instructional firing.						
Total						

V. *Other Remarks of Company Chief, of Special Importance.*
Place and date.

Name

Rank

2. Sold or returned.
    1. — lbs. lead picked up.
    2. — cartridge cases.
    3. — cartridge packets.

II. *For Revolvers.*

Received—

for — Officers	..	..	..	— rounds.
„ — under-officers		..	..	— „
„ — men ..	..	..	..	— „
„ — returned cartridge cases, &c.				— „
Total		..	..	— rounds.

Expenditure.

For firing exercises	..	..	— rounds.
„ trial shots	..	..	.. — „
Complete miss-fires	..	..	— „
Unserviceable	..	..	.. — „
Total	..	..	— rounds.
Surplus	..	..	— rounds.

Returned.
    1. — cartridge cases.
    2. — cartridge packets.

The weight of the recovered lead is included in that shown under rifle ammunition.

Place
Date

Name

Rank

Form 5.

MUSKETRY REPORT
Of the —— Battalion.
  „ —— Regiment.
  „ —— Infantry Brigade.
  „ —— Division.

88

1.Under obligation to complete all the target practice exercises (No. 4 of company musketry report).					2.No. of privates who have fulfilled the conditions of exercises for which conditions are prescribed.			3.Privates transferred.		4.Expenditure of ammu- and men serving				
Officers.	Under-officers.	Men.			I.	II.	III.	IInd to Ist.	IIIrd to IInd.	Target practice.	Special exercises.		Prize shooting.	Trial shots.
		I.	II.	III.	*a.*Total.*b.*Calculated as a percentage on the number of privates shown in column 1. Class.			*a.*Total.*b.*Calculated as a percentage on the number of privates of the IInd or IIIrd class shown in column 1. Class.			Officers.	Under-officers and men.		
		Class.												

a. ... *a.*
b. ... *b.*

Place and date

89

4. nition for Officers, under-officers with the colours.					5.	6.	7.	8.	9.
Field firing.		Musketry inspection.			Expenditure of ammunition by Officers, under-officers and men of the "on leave" category, scholastic candidates, &c.	Total.	Complete miss-fires.	Unserviceable cartridges.	Any important remarks by battalion commander and higher authorities, including statements as to time and place of field firing by formed bodies and musketry inspection in the field.
Individual.	In formed bodies.	Individual.	In open field.	Instructional firing.					
									Name Rank

XI. PROVING RIFLES AND REVOLVERS AND TESTING AMMUNITION.

§ 60. PROVING THE RIFLE. M/71. 84.

If a rifle has undergone any repair, which, according to existing regulations, requires that it should be proved anew, it will first be ascertained whether the bottoms of all the sight notches are in the same perpendicular plane. If this is the case, the proof by firing is carried out by the company. The armourer or an armourer's assistant will, on application, be placed at the disposal of the company, and will if necessary adjust the fore-sight.

For proof firing, which is to be carried out in favourable weather, only perfectly reliable shots are to be employed, and every necessary precaution is to be taken to ensure the greatest possible accuracy of shooting and to avoid errors of aiming. The sighting apparatus must be provided with sufficient cover and protected from dazzling sunshine; the screw in the case and the breech screw pin must be properly screwed home, and the rings must not pinch.

The ring target will be used, horizontal pencil lines being drawn across the whole surface at the height of the outer boundary of the 7th ring above and below the bullseye, and these lines connected by pencil lines 3·14 inches to the right and left of the perpendicular middle line of the target, so as to describe a rectangle 23·6 inches high and 6·29 inches wide within the man's breadth.

The firing is executed at 100 metres (109·3 yards). The firer sits behind an ordinary table of sufficient size, lays the rifle on a sand bag placed before him on the table, and fires 5 shots consecutively, without waiting for marking between them, using the standing sight, aiming at the bottom of the lower cross-patch, and resting his elbows.

A rifle fulfils the conditions to be exacted at proof firing if 4 out of the 5 shots give hits inside the rectangle described on the man's breadth and all 5 shots are within the two horizontal pencil lines.

In doubtful cases the proof will be repeated with other firers.

If the rifle cannot be made to shoot accurately, it will be sent for examination or repair to the nearest small-arm manufactory.

A similar mode of procedure will be adopted if a rifle, without having been repaired, is tested by firing at the "band."

§ 61. PROVING THE REVOLVER. M/83.

If a revolver misses the figure target repeatedly, it will be proved by being fired by a reliable shot, in doubtful cases by several firers, who will fire 5 rounds at 20 metres (21·8 yards), with rest. For this purpose an ordinary table of sufficient size is used, with a sand bag lying on it, on which the firer, who sits behind the table, places the revolver.

If an average of 5 hits is not reached with each 5 shots at the figure target, the revolver is to be sent to the Erfurt small-arm manufactory for examination. For the preceding purpose surplus ammunition is to be used in the first instance. If there is none, or if it is insufficient, the necessary supply of supplementary cartridges must be demanded through the usual channel.

§ 62. Testing Ball Cartridge for Rifles and Revolvers as Regards their Serviceableness for Practice Purposes.

1. *In General.*

If the ball cartridges issued for purposes of exercise behave in such a way as to have a really bad effect on the musketry instruction of the troops, they will be submitted to a special test as to their serviceableness by a committee nominated by the regimental commander, or, in the case of an isolated battalion, by the battalion commander.

2. *Grounds for Objection.*

The ammunition is to be objected to as unserviceable in the following cases :—

a. If the number of cartridges which cannot be loaded or miss fire exceeds 2 per cent.

b. If there are any cartridges that hang fire, *i.e.*, if the sound of the percussion of the striker (or hammer) does not coincide with that of the explosion, but the latter follows the former after a certain interval. As soon as this defect is noticed for certain, the firing exercises with the lot of cartridges in question are at once to be suspended.

c. If cartridges present themselvs which explode, but do so with a feeble sound, and the bullets strike the target very low or fall in front of it.

d. If in target practice the accuracy of the cartridges is so faulty that it appears doubtful whether the exercises prescribed can be shot off with the ammunition at disposal.

Cartridges are further to be considered as unserviceable for the rifle if during firing the bases of more than 0·5 per cent. of the cartridge cases tear off, or the cases crack across or lengthwise so that there is difficulty in extracting them, and the firer is inconvenienced by the powder gases.

3. *Composition of the Testing Committee.*

As soon as a report is received by the regimental or battalion commander, accompanied by the musketry books confirming the existence of the objectionable circumstances, he appoints a committee to test the ammunition.

This examination extends on each occasion to the whole of the ammunition of the same lot.

The committee consists of 3 officers, viz., of a captain as president, an inspector of small arms and a lieutenant (if possible one who has been trained at the school of musketry). Five men, reliable shots, and five normal-shooting rifles or revolvers are placed at the disposal of the committee. A previous inspection of the working of the lock will be held.

The rifles are to be provided with new spiral springs.

The sighting arrangements of the weapons used must be properly provided with cover.

4. Mode of Conducting the Several Tests.

a. Testing as to Facility of Loading.

The testing of cartridges said to be incapable of being loaded is effected by inserting a separate lot of 100 cartridges into each rifle, or 40 cartridges into each revoler.

b. Testing Miss-fires, Hang-fires, and Cracked Cases.

The examination is made by firing at a butt.

Fifty shots are fired separately twice from each rifle (20 twice from each revolver), and the result of each shot noted. If miss-fire cartridges present themselves among those that are objected to as hang-fires, the chamber of the rifle is not to be opened at once, but only after 10 seconds delay, or, in the case of the revolver, the latter is to be kept at the present for 10 seconds after pulling off.

In testing rifle ammunition for cracked cases, the place and year of manufactory, and the number of ring-shaped marks stamped on the surface showing the number of times they have been used again, should be noted.

c. Testing for Accuracy.

If the ammunition is complained of on account of feeble report or want of accuracy of hitting, it is tested by firing for accuracy, 250 rifle cartridges, or 100 revolver cartridges, taken from the several barrels, being used.

5. Mode of Conducting the Shooting.

For Rifle Ammunition.

The firing will take place at 100 metres distance at a section target marked with equilateral rectangles 1·96 inches in the side, using the standing sight and adopting the mode of presenting prescribed for proving the rifle (*See* § 60). In the middle of the target, as shown in Fig. 15, is a perpendicular band, 1·96 inches wide, which ends 23·6 inches above the lower edge of the target, and below the band and connected with it is a transverse patch 5·9 inches long and 3·9 inches deep, serving as point of aim. The point of aim is the bottom of the patch in continuation of the band.

It is allowable to let the individual marksmen fire a few comparative rounds for their guidance before the shooting for diagrams of shot-groupings commences. In other respects the firing will be conducted as follows :—

Each man shoots a shot diagram (*Trefferbild*) of 50 shots with the same rifle, the individual shots not being marked. After each 10 shots there is a pause, during which the hits are copied on the shot diagram ($\frac{1}{10}$th of the real size) and the bullet holes on the target are covered up. At the same time the barrel is perfectly cooled by pouring water through it and wiped dry.

For each shot diagram of a rifle the mean point of impact of the 50 shots is ascertained as follows:—25 bullet holes are counted from above downwards and a horizontal red line drawn half way between the 25th and 26th hole; similarly 25 holes are counted from left to right, and a vertical red line drawn between the 25th and 26th hole. The point of intersection of these two lines is the mean point of impact.

Around the mean point of impact, two rectangles are described by means of red lines, a small one 7·8 inches high and

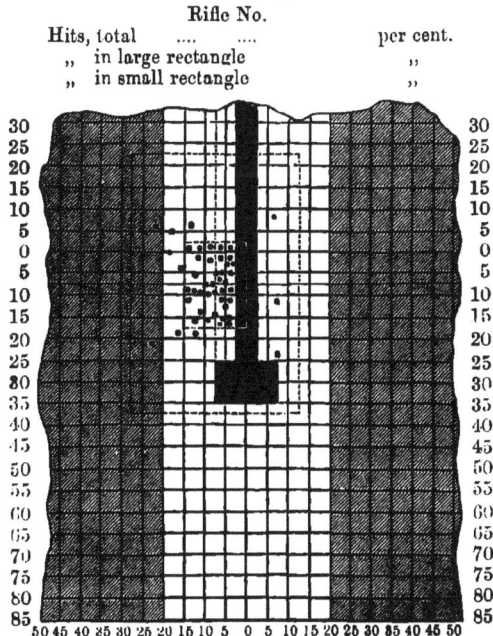

FIG. 15.—Target Diagram No.
Rifle No.

Hits, total   ....   per cent.
  „   in large rectangle   „
  „   in small rectangle   „

5·9 inches wide, and a larger one 23·6 inches high and 15·7 inches wide, so placed that the centres of the rectangles coincide with the mean point of impact. For each shot diagram the total number of hits and the number of hits within the large and small rectangle respectively will be ascertained (*See* Fig. 15).

If in the 5 shot diagrams a total of 100 per cent. hits is not shown on the target, and if, of those shown, on the average, 98 per cent. are not marked on the large rectangle and 60 per cent. on the small one, the ammunition is unserviceable. Otherwise the proof firing is repeated, and the ammunition is only to be considered serviceable if again at this second firing the above figures are reached. If that is not the case, the ammunition is noted as unserviceable.

For Revolver Ammunition.

The firing will take place at 25 metres (27·3 yards) at a ring target marked with equilateral rectangles 1·96 inches in the side, the band, bullseye and rings being omitted; the mode of presenting is that prescribed for proving the revolver (*see* § 61). From the centre of the target, with a radius of 7·8 inches, a circle is described, and under it in the middle of the target is a patch, 5·9 inches high and 3·9 inches wide, serving for point of aim. (*See* Fig. 16.)

FIG. 16.—Target Diagram No.

Revolver No.

Hits, total .... per cent.
„ in man's breadth .... „
„ within circle .... „

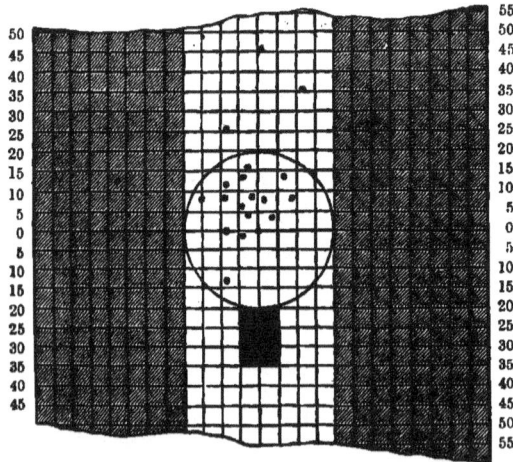

The point aimed at is the bottom of this patch.

Each man shoots a shot diagram of 20 shots with the same revolver, the individual shots not being marked. After 10 shots there is pause, during which the barrel is perfectly cooled by pouring water through it and then wiped dry. After 20 shots the hits are copied on the shot diagram ($\frac{1}{10}$th of real size). For each shot diagram the total number of hits and the hits on the man's breadth and within the circle are to be ascertained.

If in the 5-shot diagrams a total of 100 per cent. hits is not shown on the target, and on the average 90 per cent. hits on a man's breadth and 80 per cent. within the circle, the ammunition is marked as unserviceable. Otherwise the proof firing is repeated, and the ammunition is only to be considered serviceable if again at this second firing the above figures are reached. If that is not the case, the ammunition is noted as unserviceable.

6. *Report of Proceedings.*

A report on the results of the trials is to be drawn up, and a decision as to the unserviceableness of the ammunition applied for at the War Ministry (General War Department) if the defects stated in the original report are established by the trials.

7. *Replacement of Ammunition Expended or Declared Unserviceable.*

The troop commanders will be applied to for the replacement of the ammunition used for proof firings, and of that declared unserviceable, the proceedings being attached. Army Corps commanders will authorise the issue of ammunition necessary to ensure the exercises being carried out without interruption. The ammunition objected to remains with the corps until the War Ministry, after examination of the proceedings, &c., has decided as to the serviceableness or rejection of the ammunition objected to, and the replacement of the same and of the cartridges used in the trials.

BRONSART v. SCHELLENDORFF.

Berlin, 22nd February, 1887.
War Ministry.

APPENDICES.

APPENDIX A.

Profile of the Breastworks or Shelter-trenches used in Target Practice (§ 9, 2 of the Musketry Instructions), Field Firing and Instructional Firing of Infantry.

As a general rule, the measurements will be in accordance with those given in the following figure :—

APP. A, FIG. 1.

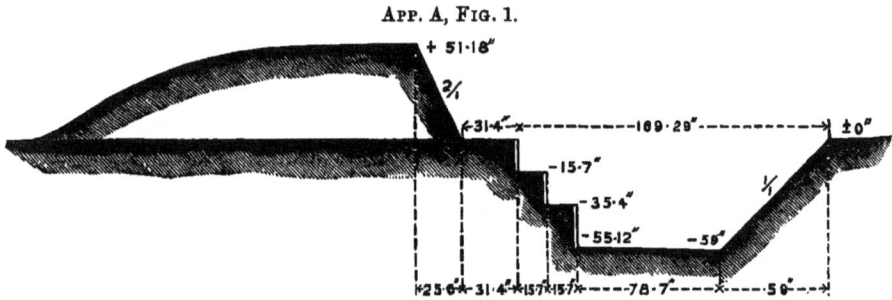

The following remarks must, however, be attended to :—

1. According to the object in view, it is immaterial whether the work is sunk more or less, or not at all, in the ground ; the only matter of importance is the correctness of form of those parts which affect the position of the firer and his rifle. Consequently, the mode of executing the work will be governed, especially on rifle ranges, by local circumstances.

The construction must leave some margin for the difference in size of the men. If there is not sufficient room to allow of variety in the height of the profile (on firing ranges), care must be taken that the men are able, by laying down sods, &c., to arrange a standing-place suitable to the size, &c., of their bodies.

3. Especially must it be left to the choice of the individual firer whether he will avail himself of a step cut out of the interior slope of the parapet for the purpose of supporting his arm, and holding his ammunition in readiness. Steps of this sort, which the firer would have to make for himself in real warfare, must be permanently made on some part of the parapets provided on firing ranges.

The following figures are given as a guide :—

App. A, Fig. 2.

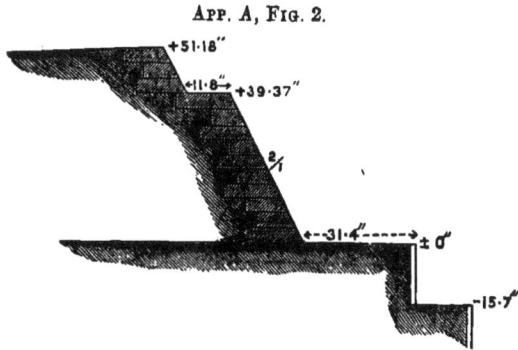

App. A, Fig. 3.

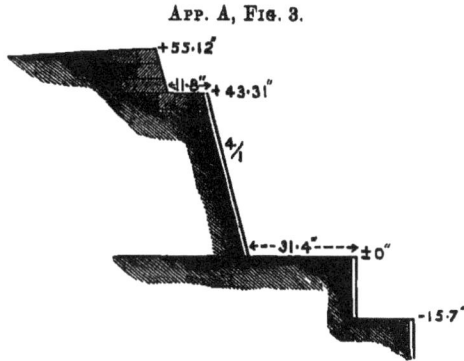

APPENDIX B.

Rests for fixing the Position of the Rifle when firing during Darkness or in a Fog.

Regulations regarding the Use of Rests.

Rests are **used** in siege warfare, both by the defender and assailant, whenever a considerable extent of ground is required to be rendered unsafe by means of infantry fire during darkness or in misty weather. (Positions in which a large number of men is known or supposed to be collected for the purpose of executing works, or covering their construction, transporting material, &c.) They enable the rifle to be kept approximately in a given position and direction, and guarantee a comparatively favourable fire effect even during a long-continued musketry attack.

The construction of rests and the mode of using them must

(3269)   G be simple, in order that they may, in case of necessity, be made on a large scale from the material to be found on the spot, and that the men may be quickly accustomed to their use.

1. For the rest with a base-board (Figs. 1 and 2), a bed is made on the top of the parapet in the direction of fire, and as level as possible. The soil set at liberty in doing this is sub-

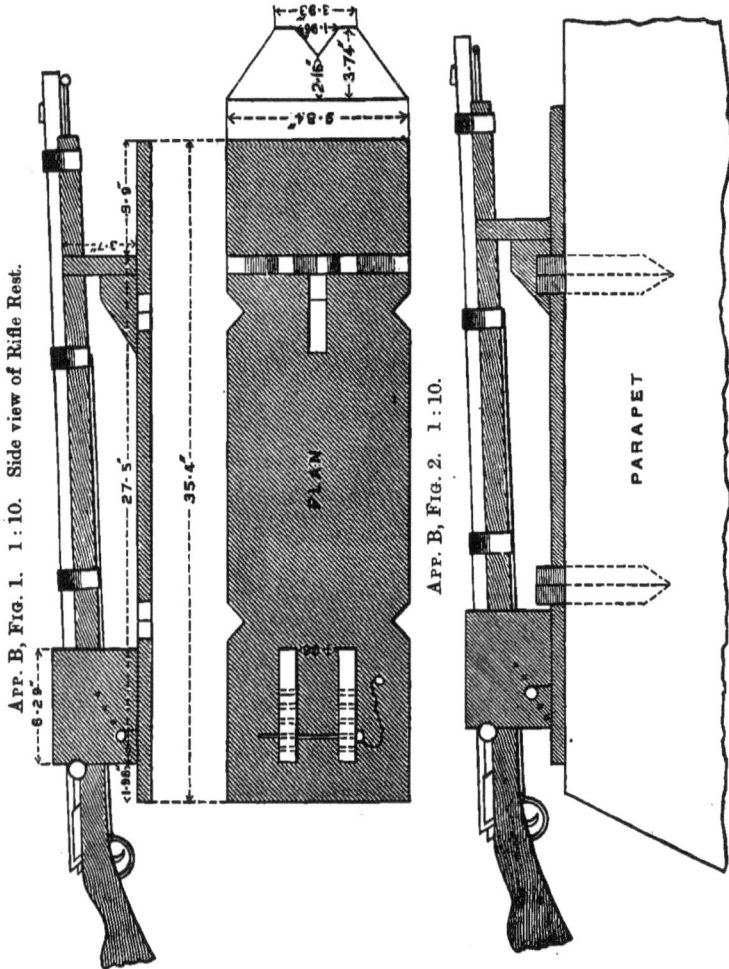

sequently used for fixing the rest. Before fire is opened, each rest must be accurately trained. To this end, the rifle is first placed in the rest, so far forward that the knob of the bolt is close up to the right-hand cheek of the rear bracket; it is then directed upon a given point of the ground to be covered with fire, with the sight raised according to the distance, and is fixed at the right elevation by means of the pin (strong nail or wire-tack), which can be inserted at different heights.

If the graduated holes in the cheeks of the bracket are not sufficient to get the exact elevation, the bed for the base-board must be lowered or raised to the extent required. After being adjusted, the rests must as far as possible be secured against being put out of position, by being weighted with soil and fixed with pegs in the notches at the sides of the board.

2. The arrangement of the rest formed of two separate pickets (Fig. 3) is on the same general principle as explained above in 1, with the difference that the elevation is obtained only by driving the pickets more or less deeply into the soil, and the rifle is placed so far forward that the trigger-guard is close up to the rear picket.

App. B, Fig. 3.   1 : 10.   A, Rear Picket.   B, Front Picket.

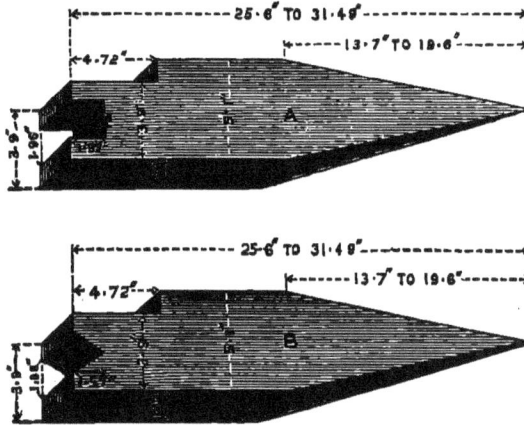

3. For using the rests by night, it will often be necessary not to fix them on the parapets, or arrange the rifles on them, until dusk. This still admits of aiming, but hides the head of the man engaged in the operation.

4. In firing the rifle, the man, as a rule, stands upright, leaning as much as possible with his left side on the interior slope of the parapet, and pressing his right shoulder to the butt so as to receive the recoil, while with his left hand he keeps the rifle in its proper position by grasping the butt as in "firing lying down with rest." The rifle can also be fired in a kneeling or stooping position, but in that case the recoil must be received with the left hand.

Under no circumstances is the firer to be permitted to withdraw the rifle under cover for the purpose of loading, as the rest is very likely to be shifted from its proper position in drawing the rifle back or pushing it forward. On the contrary, he must stand upright every time he requires to load his weapon.

5. In firing with the rifle M/71 the empty cartridge case will

be removed by means of a chip of wood, which each man has by him on the rest.

6. In order to ensure any fire effect whatever, it is absolutely necessary that the re-loaded rifle should after every shot be replaced in exactly the same position in which it was before the first shot was fired.

7. If the field should happen to be lighted up at any time by artificial light, or owing to the mist temporarily clearing off, the direction of the rest must be looked at, and, if necessary, corrected.

APPENDIX C.

Cover for Men firing in Siege Warfare.

In siege warfare, cover for the exposed parts of men firing from trenches can be obtained by using steel mantlets or shelter trench loopholes.

1. Steel Mantlets.

These consist of bullet-proof steel plates of the form represented below. In using it, the firer fixes the mantlet on the parapet near the interior crest, with its lower edge sunk a little way in the soil. For the purpose of practising firing from behind mantlets, it is sufficient to fix a board of similar shape, and not more than 0·39 inch thick, on the parapet.

APP. C, FIG. 1.   1 : 10.

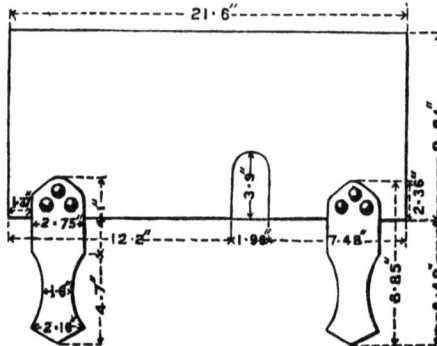

2. Shelter Trench Loopholes.

These consist of wooden or metal-plate pipes from 2 feet 7½ inches to 2 feet 9½ inches long, 3·9 inches wide (inside) at the front end and 7 inches at the rear end, embedded in a bank of earth, 15·7 inches thick at the top, which is placed on the top of the parapet. The interior slope of this superimposed bank must be revetted, and for this purpose sand-bags are most suitable.

The following figures will serve as a guide for the construction of loopholes of this description. Metal-plate loopholes should be made in the form of round conical pipes by riveting the plate.

APP. C, FIG. 2.   1 : 25.   Section.

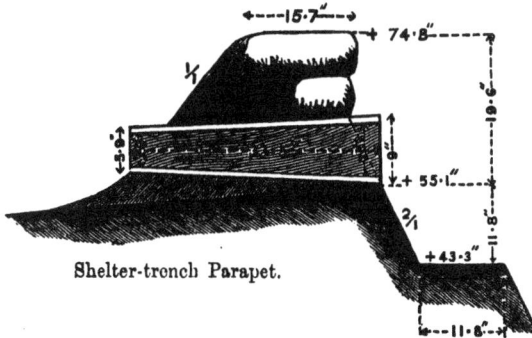

Shelter-trench Parapet.

APP. C, FIG. 3.   Inside Elevation.

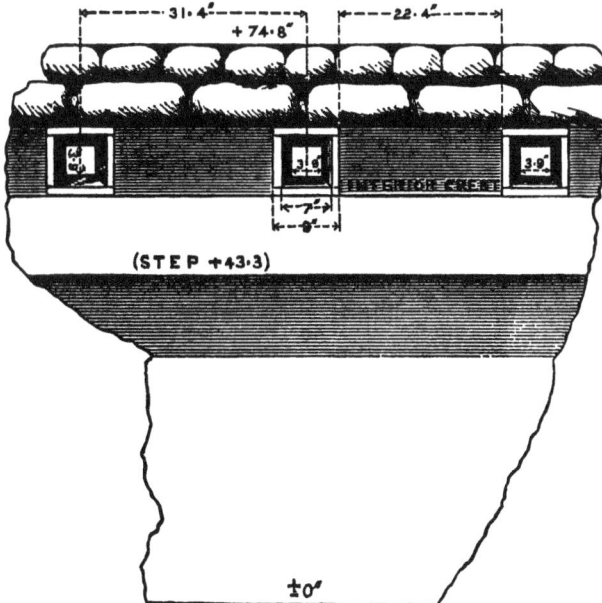

(STEP +43.3)

FINIS.

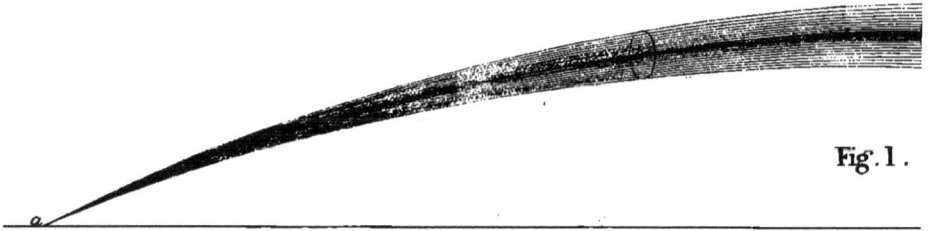

Fig. 1.

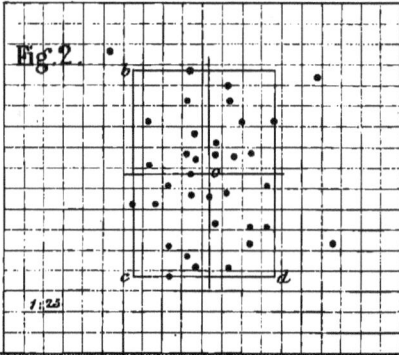

Fig. 2.

1:25

b.c. Vertical dispersion for all shots ⎫ After deducting a
c.d. Horizontal " " " ⎬ few wild shots.

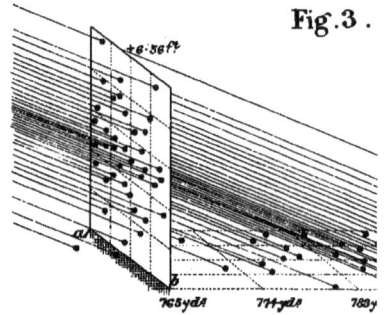

Fig. 3.

+6·86ft

765yds   714yds   760y

Fig. 5.

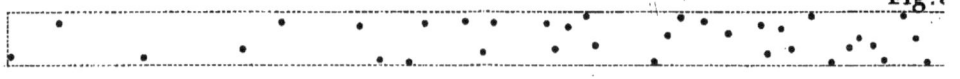

Fig. 5

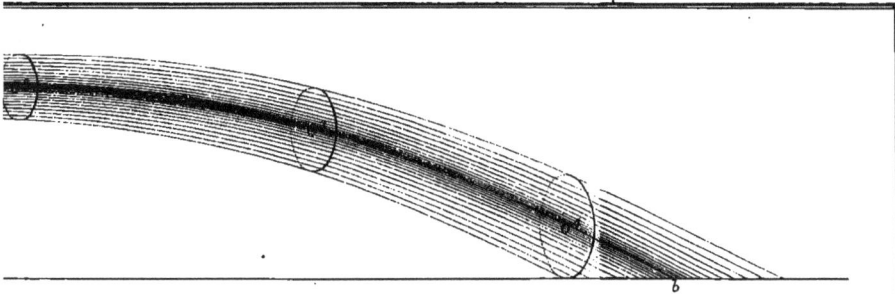

Fig. 4.

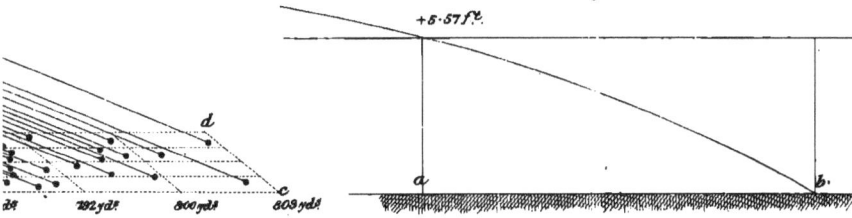

+8·57 f.ᵗ

d

c

292 yds.   800 yds.   803 yds.

a   b.

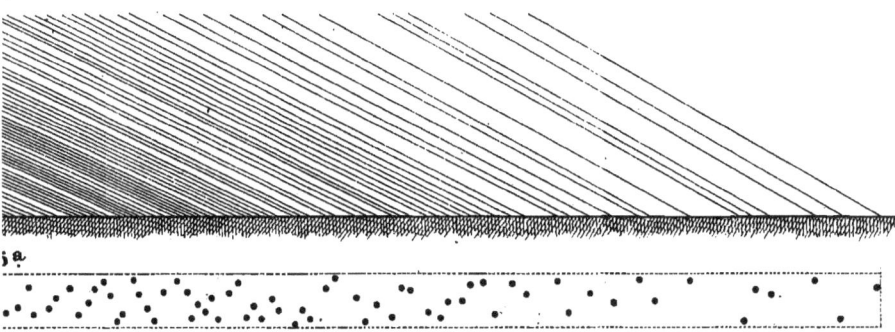

Judd & Cᵒ Lᵗᵈ Lith. 73 & 75, Farringdon Rᵈ & Doctors Commons.   728. 8/88.

SUPPLEMENT

TO TRANSLATION OF

THE MUSKETRY INSTRUCTIONS

FOR THE

GERMAN INFANTRY

OF

1887.

Containing all the Alterations made in the " Schiessvorschrift " of 1889, consequent on the adoption of the Rifle of 1888.

PREPARED IN THE INTELLIGENCE DIVISION, WAR OFFICE,

BY

COLONEL C. W. BOWDLER BELL,

AND PUBLISHED BY PERMISSION OF E. S. MITTLER AND SON, BERLIN.

NOTE BY TRANSLATOR.

The "Schiessvorschrift" of 1887, of which a translation was issued by the Intelligence Division of the War Office in 1889, contained the Musketry Regulations adapted for the rifle known in Germany as M. /71-84. This weapon was a modification of the Mauser, /71 pattern, the chief peculiarities being a repeating arrangement (the cartridges being contained in a cylinder under the barrel) and the reduction of the calibre to ·433 inch.

The "Schiessvorschrift" of 1889, dated 21st November, appeared at the beginning of the present year, and is being issued to Army Corps in succession, as they receive the rifle now definitely adopted, and which is known as Rifle 88. These regulations may be said to differ from those of 1887 chiefly in respect of the modifications in musketry training necessitated by the alterations in the mechanism, ballistic properties, and tactical uses of the new weapon; some changes have also been made in the arrangement of the paragraphs, and the instructions for fire discipline and direction of fire have been transferred to the "Infantry Drill Regulations."

A complete list of the corrections which must be made in the translation of the "Schiessvorschrift" of 1887, above referred to, in order to make it correspond to the 1889 edition, will be found below; it may, however, be of interest to give here a brief outline of the most important changes brought about by the introduction of the rifle 88.

The new weapon, which has a calibre of 7·8 mm. (0·307 in.), is distinguished as a multiple loader (Mehrlader), and is not considered to be a magazine rifle. The term "magazin" is no longer used in the musketry or drill regulations, the receptacle for holding the charge of cartridges being now called a "Kasten" (*lit.* box).* The charge consists of a bundle of 5 cartridges held together by a light steel ribbon, termed the "Rahmen" (frame or holder), which is inserted from above into the receptacle. As all the cartridges issued to the troops are in these bundles of 5, the use of the weapon as a single loader is not contemplated in warfare: it may, however, be mentioned, that when there is no "frame" in the receptacle, it is possible to load with a single cartridge, and this may be done for trial shots, &c. Omitting minor details the principal changes in the new "Musketry Regulations" are as follows:—

* The term "magazine" will, however, be retained in the following translation.

The matter is no longer arranged in long paragraphs, but in short ones, numbered consecutively throughout the book.

From the omission of the statements which appeared in the 1887 edition, that high temperatures affect the shooting powers of new rifles, and that the efficiency of powder diminishes the longer it is in store, it may be gathered that great confidence is felt in the superiority both of the new rifle and of the new and almost smokeless chemical powder.

The vast improvement in the ballistic properties of the new arm may, to some extent, be gathered from the following comparison with the rifle M. /71-84, now being replaced:—

Sighting to 2,241·8 yards, instead of 1,749·8 yards.

Velocity of bullet, 82 feet from muzzle, 2,034 feet, instead of 1,427 feet.

Extreme range 4,155 yards with an elevation of 32°, instead of 3,281 yards with an elevation of 35°.

The flatness of trajectory may be illustrated by the fact that with the 800 metre sight the mean height of trajectory at 765·5 yards is 9·186 feet, instead of 16·4 feet.

The increased accuracy of fire is shown by the vertical dispersion at 800 metres, now 6·7 feet instead of 9·1 feet, while the horizontal dispersion at that distance is only 3·6 feet instead of 6·9 feet.

As to penetrating power, 17·7 inches of dry fir are pierced at 437 yards, as against 6·9 inches at 328 yards. Steel plates ·315 inch thick are not affected beyond 55 yards. Earthen parapets to afford protection to infantry must be at least 29·5 inches thick. Thin brick walls give but imperfect protection.

The old band target is abolished, and the ring target is now plain white, with a central vertical black band and a bullseye. The cross patches and man's-breadth formerly on this target have disappeared. The discontinuance of the man's-breadth (as pointed out by a recent writer in the "Militär-Wochenblatt") results from the consideration that fire effect in future warfare will be influenced more by deviations of the bullet above and below the object than by lateral deflections; for at distances of 400 metres and over, the horizontal dispersion with the new rifle is only about two-thirds of what it was with the rifle of 1884. Objects on the battle field will generally be low lines, and hence the necessity of training the men to pay more attention to the vertical than to the lateral placing of their bullets.

In the instructions for aiming standing in the 1887 edition, it was laid down that the rifle should be directed, in the first instance, at a point about half a yard below the point to be aimed at, and gradually raised. In the present regulations, on the contrary, the firer is instructed, in all positions of aiming, to direct his rifle at once towards the point of aim, there or thereabouts; but aiming slightly below the point and gradually raising the rifle is also permitted. Formerly the horizontal position of the backsight before firing was verified by both eyes; it is in future to be ascertained by looking at the sight with the right eye only.

Consequent on the extended range of the new rifle, the requirements in judging distance have been considerably increased. Privates are expected to estimate distances accurately up to 656 yards (formerly 437 yards), and must be practised in judging from 656 to 1,093 (formerly 875) yards; while officers, non-commissioned officers, and intelligent men, are expected to be able to judge up to 1,093 yards (formerly 875), and are to practise judging even longer distances.

Distances are now classified as follows:—

Short, up to 656 yards; formerly 437 yards.
Medium, from 656 to 1,093 yards; formerly 437 to 875 yards.
Long, over 1,093 yards; formerly over 875 yards.

The conditions required to be fulfilled in target practice are much more exacting than before, the surface on which shots count being greatly reduced in extent.

Special rewards of merit have been instituted for officers and non-commissioned officers of infantry, the best shot among the former in each Army Corps receiving a sword from the Emperor, and the best shot among the latter a watch.

Owing to the increased accuracy of the new rifle, the distances at which there is a probability of each shot hitting certain objects are greatly extended, being as follows:—

Up to 273·4 yards (formerly 218·7) against all objects.
Up to 382·7 yards (formerly 273·4) against a single man kneeling.
Up to 546·8 yards (formerly 382·7) against a file kneeling.
Up to 656·1 yards (formerly 492·1) against a single horseman.

With regard to sights, only one sight is now used, as a rule, up to 875 yards (formerly up to 656 yards only); beyond that distance 2 sights, differing by about 110 yards, will generally be used.

The above are the chief points of general interest in the new "Musketry Regulations." A thorough knowledge of the changes brought about by the introduction of the new rifle can only be acquired by a comparison of the two editions of the "Schiessvorschrift," which the following pages are designed to facilitate, and by a study of the "Infantry Drill Regulations of 1889," in which the manual and firing exercises, and directions for the tactical employment of infantry fire will be found.

ALTERATIONS IN DETAIL.

Page 10.   Lines 28 and 29 are omitted.
Page 11.   The last 3 lines are omitted.
Page 12.   § 7 should be altered as follows :—

BALLISTIC PROPERTIES OF THE RIFLE, 88.

1. Velocity of bullet, 25 metres (82 feet) from the muzzle, on the average 620 metres (2,034 feet).

2. Extreme range about 3,800 metres (4,155 yards) with an elevation of about 32°.

3. *Mean heights of Trajectory.*   (*See table on folded sheet*).

4. *Accuracy.*

Distance in metres	50	100	150	200	250	300	350	400
,, yards ..	54·68	109·36	164·04	218·72	273·4	328·08	382·77	437·45
Vertical dispersion in centimetres.	6	11	17	25.	34	46	57	70
Vertical dispersion in feet.	0·197	0·361	0·557	0·820	1·115	1·509	1·870	2·296
Horizontal dispersion in centimetres.	4	10	15	20	26	30	37	42
Horizontal dispersion in feet.	0·131	0·328	0·492	0·656	0·853	0·984	1·214	1·378

Distance in metres ..	450	450	600	700	800	900	1,000
,, yards ..	492·13	546·81	656·18	765·54	874·91	984·27	1093·68
Vertical dispersion in centimetres.	85	102	140	170	206	249	298
Vertical dispersion in feet.	2·790	3·346	4·593	5·577	6·758	8·170	9·777
Horizontal dispersion in centimetres.	48	53	64	88	112	136	160
Horizontal dispersion in feet.	1·575	1·739	2·099	2·887	3·674	4·462	5·249

5. Penetration.

In wood: the bullet passes through dry fir of the following thicknesses:—

31·48 inches at 109 yards.
17·7   „   437   „
9·8   „   875   „
1·96   „   1,968   „

(*On Page* 13)—

In iron: the bullet passes through iron plates ·275 inch thick up to about 328 yards. The effect on best steel plates ·315 inch thick up to 55 yards is unimportant; beyond that distance there is no effect.

The penetration in freshly thrown up sand is about 35·4 inches at 109 yards, 19·7 at 437, 13·8 at 875, and 3·9 at 1,968.

Protection against infantry fire is afforded by earthen parapets not under 29·5 inches thick.

Thin brick walls give but imperfect protection; if several bullets hit the same spot, they penetrate.

The following table of "Grazed Zones" is added after the table of "Accuracy" (on page 12):—

Grazed Zones.

Sight used.	Height of Object.					
	0·35 m. *13·78 ins.*	0·50 *19·68*	0·85 *33·56*	1·20 *47·24*	1·70 *66·93*	2·0 *78·74*
Standing sight	Entirely grazed.					
Small flap	65 m. *213·2 ft.*	108 *354·3*	Entirely grazed.			
450-metre sight	35 *114·8*	50 *164*	104 *341·2*	Entirely grazed.		
500 „	29 *95·1*	39 *127·9*	72 *236·2*	118 *387·1*	Entirely grazed.	
600 „	19 *62·3*	29 *95·1*	48 *157·5*	72 *236·2*	111 *364·1*	143 *469·1*
700 „	15 *49·2*	20 *65·6*	33 *108·2*	50 *164*	75 *246*	91 *298·6*
800 „	10 *32·8*	15 *49·2*	25 *82*	38 *124·7*	54 *177·1*	66 *216·5*
900 „	9 *29·5*	13 *42·6*	21 *68·9*	30 *98·4*	44 *144·4*	52 *170·6*

3. Mean Heights of Trajectory in Metres and Feet*

Sight used.	50 / 164	100 / 328	150 / 492	200 / 656	250 / 820	300 / 984	350 / 1148	400 / 1312	450 / 1476	500 / 1640	550 / 1804	600 / 1968	650 / 2132	700 / 2296	750 / 2460	800 / 2624	850 / 2788	900 / 2952	950 / 3116	1000 / 3280
Standing sight	0·1 / 0·328	0·2 / 0·656	0·2 / 0·656	0 / 0	−0·3 / 0·984															
Small flap	0·2 / 0·656	0·4 / 1·312	0·5 / 1·640	0·6 / 1·968	0·5 / 1·640	0·3 / 0·984	0 / 0	−0·5 / −1·640												
450-metre sight	0·4 / 1·312	0·7 / 2·296	0·9 / 2·952	1·1 / 3·609	1·1 / 3·609	1·1 / 3·609	0·9 / 2·952	0·5 / 1·640	0 / 0	−0·7 / −2·296										
500 ,,	0·4 / 1·312	0·8 / 2·624	1·1 / 3·609	1·4 / 4·593	1·5 / 4·921	1·5 / 4·921	1·4 / 4·593	1·1 / 3·609	0·6 / 1·968	0 / 0	−0·8 / −2·624									
550 ,,	0·5 / 1·640	1·0 / 3·281	1·4 / 4·593	1·7 / 5·577	1·9 / 6·233	2·0 / 6·562	1·9 / 6·233	1·7 / 5·577	1·3 / 4·265	0·8 / 2·624	0 / 0	−1·0 / −3·281								
600 ,,	0·6 / 1·968	1·1 / 3·609	1·6 / 5·249	2·0 / 6·562	2·3 / 7·546	2·5 / 8·202	2·5 / 8·202	2·4 / 7·874	2·1 / 6·889	1·6 / 5·249	0·9 / 2·953	0 / 0	−1·1 / −3·609							
650 ,,		1·3 / 4·265		2·4 / 7·874		3·0 / 9·843		3·1 / 10·170		2·5 / 8·202		1·1 / 3·609	0 / 0	−1·3 / −4·265						
700 ,,		1·5 / 4·921		2·7 / 8·858		3·5 / 11·483		3·8 / 12·467		3·4 / 11·155		2·2 / 7·218	1·2 / 3·937	0 / 0	−1·5 / −4·921					
800 ,,		1·9 / 6·233		3·5 / 11·483		4·7 / 15·420		5·4 / 17·717		5·4 / 17·717		4·6 / 15·099		2·8 / 9·186	1·6 / 5·249	0 / 0	−1·9 / −6·233			
900 ,,		2·3 / 7·546		4·4 / 14·436		6·1 / 20·013		7·2 / 23·622		7·6 / 24·934		7·3 / 23·950		6·0 / 19·685		3·6 / 11·811	2·0 / 6·562	0 / 0	−2·3 / −7·546	
1000 ,,		2·8 / 9·186		5·4 / 17·717		7·6 / 24·934		9·2 / 30·184		10·1 / 33·137		10·2 / 33·465		9·4 / 30·840		7·5 / 24·606		4·4 / 14·436	2·4 / 7·874	0 / 0
1100 ,,		3 / 9·843		6 / 19·685		9 / 29·528		11 / 36·090		13 / 42·652		13 / 42·652		13 / 42·652		12 / 39·371		9 / 29·528		5 / 16·405
1200 ,,		4 / 13·124		8 / 26·247		11 / 36·090		14 / 45·933		16 / 52·494		17 / 55·775		17 / 55·775		16 / 52·494		14 / 45·933		11 / 36·090
1300 ,,		5 / 16·405		9 / 29·528		13 / 42·635		16 / 52·494		19 / 62·337		21 / 68·899		21 / 68·899		21 / 68·899		20 / 65·618		17 / 55·775
1400 ,,		5 / 16·405		10 / 32·809		15 / 49·213		19 / 62·337		22 / 72·180		25 / 82·022		26 / 85·304		27 / 88·584		26 / 85·304		24 / 78·741
1500 ,,		6 / 19·685		12 / 39·371		17 / 55·775		22 / 72·180		26 / 85·304		29 / 95·146		31 / 101·706		32 / 104·989		32 / 104·989		31 / 101·706
1600 ,,		7 / 22·966		13 / 42·652		19 / 62·337		25 / 82·022		29 / 96·146		33 / 108·270		37 / 121·393		39 / 127·955		39 / 127·955		39 / 127·953
1700 ,,		8 / 26·247		15 / 49·213		22 / 72·180		28 / 91·865		34 / 111·550		38 / 124·674		42 / 137·798		45 / 147·640		47 / 154·198		47 / 154·201
1800 ,,		8 / 26·247		17 / 55·775		24 / 78·741		31 / 101·706		38 / 124·674		44 / 144·360		48 / 157·483		52 / 170·607		55 / 180·449		56 / 183·730
1900 ,,		9 / 29·528		18 / 59·056		27 / 88·584		35 / 114·831		43 / 141·079		49 / 160·764		55 / 180·449		60 / 196·854		63 / 206·697		65 / 213·255
2000 ,,		10 / 32·809		20 / 65·618		30 / 98·427		39 / 127·955		48 / 157·483		55 / 180·440		62 / 203·416		67 / 219·890		72 / 236·235		75 / 246·067
2050 ,,		11 / 36·090		21 / 68·899		32 / 104·989		41 / 134·517		50 / 164·045		58 / 190·289		65 / 213·252		71 / 232·944		76 / 249·349		80 / 262·471

* The figures in small type show feet; the neare[...]

Distances.

1050	1100	1150	1200	1250	1300	1350	1400	1450	1500	1550	1600	1650	1700	1750	1800	1850	1900	1950	2000	2050
3444	3608	3772	3936	4100	4264	4428	4592	4756	4920	5084	5248	5413	5577	5741	5905	6069	6233	6397	6561	6725
−2·7 −8·853																				
3 9·843	0 0	−3 −9·843																		
	6 19·685	3 9·843	0 0	−4 −13·124																
	13 43·653		7 23·966	4 13·124	0 0	−4 −13·124														
	20 65·618		15 49·213		9 29·528	5 16·405	0 0	−5 −16·405												
	28 91·865		24 78·741		18 59·086		10 32·809	5 16·405	0 0	−6 −19·685										
	37 121·393		33 108·270		28 91·865		21 68·899		11 36·090	6 19·685	0 0	−7 −22·966								
	46 150·921		43 141·079		39 127·955		32 104·989		24 74·741		13 42·652	7 22·966	0 0	−8 −26·247						
	56 183·730		54 177·169		50 164·045		45 147·640		37 121·393		27 88·584		15 49·213	8 26·247	0 0	−8 −26·247				
	66 216·539		65 213·253		62 203·418		58 190·299		51 167·396		42 137·798		31 101·708		17 55·775	9 29·528	0 0	−9 −39·262		
	77 253·929		77 252·629		75 246·007		71 232·944		66 216·539		58 190·292		47 154·202		34 111·550		19 62·337	10 32·809	0 0	−10 −32·809
	82 269·034		83 272·315		82 269·034		79 259·191		78 239·800		66 216·539		56 183·730		44 144·360		28 91·865		10 32·809	0 0

t whole number in the case of distances,

Sight used.	Height of Object.					
	0·35 m. 13·78 ins.	0·50 19·68	0·85 33·56	1·20 47·24	1·70 66·93	2·0 78·74
1200-metre sight	5 16·4	8 26·2	13 42·6	18 59	23 75·5	30 98·4
1500 ,, ...	4 13·1	6 19·7	8 26·2	11 36	15 49·2	16 52·5
1800 ,, ...	3 9·8	4 13·1	7 22·9	8 26·2	11 36	14 45·9
2000 ,, ...	2 6·6	3 9·8	5 16·4	7 22·9	9 29·5	11 36

Pages 13 and 14. The Band Target there described is abolished.

Pages 14 and 15. The Ring Target is altered as follows:—
This is 66·93 inches high, and 47·24 inches broad. It is painted white.

RING TARGET.

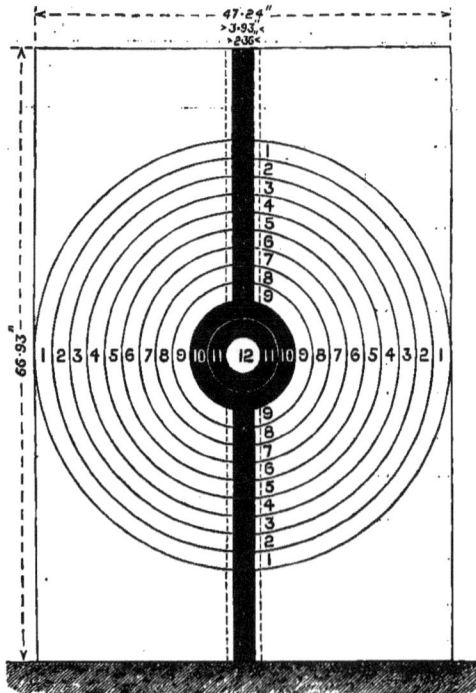

From the centre of the target 12 circles are described, and the rings so marked off are numbered 1 to 12 from without inwards. The radius of the centre circle, number 12, is 1·96 inches; the radii of the others increase by 1·96 inches each.

The rings 10 and 11 are filled in with black, and together with the 12th form the bullseye.

Down the centre of the target is drawn a perpendicular black band, 2·36 inches wide, which is not carried across the bullseye. The separation of ring 10 from the black band and from ring 11 is shown by red lines. The rings 1 to 9 can be marked with pencil where they cross the black band.

For the first exercises in target practice, an aiming surface 3·93 inches broad is to be marked by two red lines, visible only to the marker, one along each side of the black band and 0·78 inch from it. Hits on this surface are termed "band hits." The red lines are to be carried across the bullseye.

Page 16, line 11; after "brown colour," the following addition is made:—

The centre and two outermost parts may be brown, and in that case the other two parts will be white.

Mounted figure target; 78·7 inches high, and 33·5 or 66·9 inches wide, according as the rider is seen from the front or sideways. On the target is either a coloured representation of a mounted man, or the outline of one filled in with a dark colour.

Page 16, fourth line from bottom; after "suitable" the addition is made "(Compare Tables V and X of the Anleitung für den Bau von Schiessständen)"

Pages 16 and 17. § 9, on "Shooting Apparatus," is altered as follows:—In sub-paragraph 1, the words "As a preparation for shooting without rest (free-handed)" are omitted, and in place of them are substituted "For shooting standing with rest."

The whole of the remaining sub-paragraphs of this paragraph, including Figs. 9 and 10, are cancelled, and in place thereof Appendices A, B, and C, pages 96 to 101, are transferred, with the following modifications:—

Appendix A. The whole of the letter-press and figures are inserted here. In Fig. 2 the height of the interior crest may vary from 51·18″ to 59″; that of the step from 39·37″ to 47·24″. In Fig. 3 the height of the interior crest may vary from 55·12″ to 59″; that of the step from 43·31″ to 47·24″.

Appendix B. Only the figures are inserted here; the descriptive letter-press is transferred to page 68; a slight alteration is made in Figs. 1 and 2 (showing the rifle sling long), the dimensions being unaltered; the notch at the top of the rear picket in Fig. 3 is modified in section to suit the new rifle.

Appendix C. The figure showing the steel mantlet is inserted here, the description transferred to page 68. The description and figures of shelter trench loopholes are omitted altogether.

Page 18. § 12. "Ammunition." A new sub-paragraph is added between 2 and 3, as follows:—

For prize-shooting, for each officer and non-commissioned officer, at least 15 rounds.

Sub-paragraph 4 now reads "For instructional firing, at least 200 rounds."

Page 19, line 31; the words "ring target, standing position," are omitted. Line 36; after "field-firing exercises" the words "in individual firing" are added.

Page 20, line 7; the word "preparatory" is substituted for "preliminary." Line 36; after "free-handed," the following is added:—"The present in the standing position with rest, owing to the support of the rifle, prevents the firer becoming tired, and enables the instructor thoroughly to superintend the firer in every detail."

Page 21. Lines 3 and 4, and the whole of sub-paragraphs 3 and 4, are cancelled."

Page 23, eighth line from bottom; after "given point," the following is added:—"In doing this the left eye is to be closed, and the man must be accustomed, before commencing the act of aiming, to observe whether the shoulders of the back-sight are horizontal. If any men keep both their eyes open when aiming, there is no objection to their doing so."

Page 24. Lines 10 to 17 are altered as follows:—"In free-handed aiming, standing, as also in every other variety of aiming, the left eye being closed, the firer must endeavour to direct the rifle at once, approximately, at the point of aim, the horizontal position of the back-sight being at the same time observed, and the act of aiming proper is then immediately commenced. It is also permissible for the man to direct the rifle somewhat under the point of aim in the present and while aiming, and then to raise it gradually with the left hand only, without any bending of the back or hips." The sentence commencing "For example," lines 21 to 25, is omitted. Lines 10 and 11 from the bottom are omitted. 4th line from the bottom, the word "magazine" is substituted for "trigger guard."

Page 25, line 17; after the word "finger" the words are added "lies against the inner part of the under side of the trigger guard and." 8th line from bottom; after "laid" the words "with its fore part" are inserted, and in the next line the words "between the upper and middle ring" are omitted.

Page 26, lines 15 and 16; instead of "directed at first about half a metre below the mark," this now reads "at once directed at the mark."

Page 26, lines 17 to 21 have been altered as follows:—"The exact mode of presenting when lying down or kneeling, behind objects which serve for cover or as a support for the rifle, depends upon the build of the individual firer, the ground, the nature of the object aimed at, and the circumstances of the fight." Lines 24 to 26; the sentence commencing "Nearly every sort" is omitted. 20th line from bottom; "lower ring" is substituted for "middle ring." 9th line from bottom; "between the middle and lower ring" now reads "behind the lower ring." 6th and 5th lines from bottom; the left hand grasps "the magazine" instead of "the stock in front of the trigger guard."

Page 27, lines 10 and 11; the words "in which no fixed rule for the position of the left hand can be given" now read, "in which the left hand grasps the rifle as in presenting lying-down free-handed."

In sub-paragraph c the words "which affords cover from the enemy's fire" are omitted, and the following added after "fore-finger":—"Trees, even when of suitable girth, give cover only from the front, and not from the side. The mode of presenting above described will therefore be adopted only if the firer has no open field of fire when lying down or kneeling."

At the end of sub-paragraph d the sentence is added:—"It is allowable for the firer, if it gives him greater convenience in presenting, to rest his left side against the interior slope."

Page 28, lines 16 and 17; the words "and in increased measure" and "aiming ammunition" are omitted.

16th line from bottom; the words "a rifle loaded with a miss-fire cartridge, or" are omitted.

Page 29, line 11; after "loaded," add "or unlocked." The following instructions are substituted for lines 17 to 44 down to "raising the rifle":—

"The left hand, in a perfectly natural position, supports the rifle, all unnecessary exertion being avoided. Immediately after bringing in the rifle to the shoulder, the forefinger of the right hand assumes the proper feeling of the trigger, and the firer, closing the left eye, observes that the shoulders of the back sight are horizontal and then takes aim. In doing this, the rifle is directed at once as nearly as possible at the point to be aimed at, without any bending of the loins or hips. As the eye is fixed on the point to be aimed at and its direction maintained, the firer begins pressing the trigger by a gradual and almost imperceptible bending of the forefinger, so that the rifle is discharged without the firer knowing exactly when it will go off. It is also permissible for the firer, when presenting, to direct his rifle at first a little below the point to be aimed at and to raise it gradually with the left hand, without any bending of the loins or hips, the pressure of the forefinger being gradually increased so that the rifle is discharged the moment the point is reached at which it is to be directed."

Page 30. Lines 8 to 16 are altered as follows:—

"The men must learn to estimate distances up to 600 metres (656 yards)—short distances—with accuracy, and must be practised in judging from 600 to 1,000 metres (1,093·6 yards)—medium distances. Officers, non-commissioned officers, and intelligent men ought to be able to judge up to 1,000 metres, and are to practise judging longer distances. Lastly, officers ought to be able to read distances quickly and accurately from large scale maps."

Lines 19 to 21 omitted from "in doing which."

Line 25. Omit sentence commencing "On this fact."

Lines 27 to 31, now read "the latter mode presupposes that an enemy is firing with powder that is not smokeless. Distances can also be ascertained by trial shots."

Page 31, line 1; omit "rising or." Line 3, omit "great heat." Line 5, omit "on falling ground."

Lines 17 to 19 now read "non-commissioned officers and men are first to be trained to pace distances accurately."

Page 32, line 4; for 200 read 600. Lines 10 to 19 are omitted. Lines 20 to 25 now read "In the case of distances beyond 200 metres the first mentioned method is apt to lead to incorrect results, and preference is therefore to be given to the second method." Line 30; omit "side lines, *e.g.*" Line 32; omit "side." 7th line from bottom; omit "200 and."

Page 33, line 1, for "up to 800" read "beyond 600." Line 4; for "3" read "2." Line 6; for "400" read "600." Lines 13 to 25 omitted.

Page 34. Sub-paragraph 4 now stands as follows :—"Men whose short-sightedness with the right eye is certified by the medical officer, and who for any special reasons cannot aim with the left eye, shoot with glasses. If even then their sight is not sufficiently good they perform the firing exercises with glasses in the same way as the other men, but only at distances for which their sight is adapted. In the latter case the men are ineligible for musketry prizes or marksmen's badges, and cannot be promoted into higher musketry classes."

7th line from bottom; omit "so that they may have the necessary rest."

Page 35, line 7; add "Rifle slings long or short, as the company commander may direct."

Line 19; omit "where such are prescribed."

15th line from bottom; after "Commander" add "More numerous an l more difficult exercises, but not too [difficult conditions, are to be prescribed."

Page 36, line 6; for "preliminary" read "preparatory." Line 14; for "barrels" read "inside of the barrels and magazines." 9th line from bottom; the first sentence of sub-paragraph *b* now reads "His business is to see that no rifle is loaded or unlocked until the flag has been shown in the case of markers' shelters of the old sort, or, in the case of blinded or sunken shelters, until the target is visible or the signalling is completed." 4th line from bottom; omit from "and takes" to end of page.

Page 37, line 27; for "with chambers, &c." read "rifles open." Line 30; after "loads" add "(except in the 14th practice of the 3rd class, and 10th practice of the 2nd and 1st class) a full packet of cartridges." Lines 32 to 35; omit sentence "In loading, &c." 11th and 12th lines from bottom now read "If a cartridge misses fire, it will in the first instance be given another position in the chamber."

Page 38, line 1 ; omit " complete." Line 8 ; after " cross-wise " add " or " cartridge packets are damaged." Lines 10 to 14 ; omit from " He then " to " parapet " and substitute as follows :—" He then loads again and secures, but, in the case of markers' shelters of the old sort, not until the flag is again shown at the target. He then returns to the detachment and advances again, with locked rifle, to fire a round when his turn comes. He must not make ready for firing until the flag in the case of shelters of the old sort, or the target in the case of shelters of other kinds, is shown.

When the man has fired his number of rounds, he does not re-load. He removes the cartridge case, or the cartridge packet with such cartridges as may be in it, leaves the rifle open and falls in.

Loading, securing and unloading are to be performed facing the target, and, in the case of shelters of the old sort, must be completed before the markers re-appear.

In firing kneeling, lying down or behind parapets, the man may fire several shots in succession. In such cases, with shelters of the old sort, after a shot has been fired the rifle must not be opened for loading until the flag is again visible."

Line 17 ; for " drawn under cover " read " hidden."

Line 27 ; add " These cartridges, and such as are used for trial shots, can be loaded singly in the barrel without using the cartridge-packet."

Page 39, line 16; omit " as near as possible to the butt." Line 17 ; omit " on the ground, or." Lines 25 and 26 ; for " man's breadth, figure, or any part of the equipment " read " or figure target."

Page 40, lines 26 to 29 ; the following is substituted :—" The shelter may be left, in a circumspect manner, as soon as it is clearly seen with the mirror that the firing is suspended and a counter-signal has been made calling upon the marker to signal or leave the shelter. A similar procedure is adopted if special circumstances make it necessary to leave the shelter."

13th and 14th lines from bottom ; for " The shooting, &c., consequently " read " As soon as the order or signal for commence firing is given by the firing detachment, and the target is consequently shown, the firing may commence."

Page 41, lines 6 and 7 from bottom ; omit. Last three lines now read " In the ranges appropriated to one and the same body of troops one uniform system of duty must be adopted. Compare § 12 of the " Anleitung für den Bau von Schiess-ständen."

Page 42, lines 1 to 5 ; omit. Line 23 ; after " drum " add " in target practice."

Sub-paragraph 6 now reads " Rifles which are not actually in the men's hands are to be open. They must have no cartridges in the magazine. If a loaded rifle, or an opened rifle with cartridges in the magazine, is given over to any person, it must be accompanied with the words "It is loaded."

Page 43, lines 12 and 13; for 200 and 300 metres, read 250 and 350 metres respectively. The aiming table, continued on page 44 is omitted.

Page 44, 7th line from bottom; after "be" add "chiefly." 2nd to 4th lines from bottom: omit sentence "The firer, &c."

Pages 45 to 47. The following alterations have been made:—

Third Shooting Class.

1st practice	..	Ring target; 3 hits, 2 bands.
2nd ,,	..	Ring target; 3 hits, 2 bands, 2 bullseyes.
3rd ,,	..	30 points in the rings, no shot under 9.
4th ,,	..	3 hits, 24 in rings, 2 shots within 9.
5th ,,	..	27 in rings, 2 shots within 9.
6th ,,	..	3 hits, 20 in rings, 2 shots within 8.
13th ,,	..	5 hits, 25 in rings, 3 shots within 6.
14th ,,	..	Figure target, 3 figures, 5 consecutive shots within 30 seconds from the first shot, without the markers signalling between times. The exercise is to begin with only 2 cartridges in the packet.

Omit the words "in the last practice in 6" on page 45.

Second Shooting Class.

1st practice	..	Ring target, 2 bands, 3 bullseyes.
2nd ,,	..	30 in rings, no shot under 9.
3rd ,,	..	3 hits, 24 in rings, 2 shots within 9.
4th ,,	..	4 figures.
5th ,,	..	3 figures.
6th ,,	..	3 figures.
7th ,,	..	3 figures.
8th ,,	..	4 hits.
9th ,,	..	5 hits, 30 in rings, 3 shots within 7.
10th ,,	..	Figure target, 3 figures; remarks as in No. 14, 3rd class.

Omit the words "in the last practice in 7" on page 46.

First Shooting Class.

1st practice	..	Ring target, 2 bands, 3 bullseyes.
2nd ,,	..	3 bullseyes.
3rd ,,	..	26 in rings, 2 shots within 9.
5th ,,	..	3 figures.
8th ,,	..	4 hits.
9th ,,	..	5 hits, 35 in rings, 3 shots within 8.
10th ,,	..	Figure target, 4 figures; remarks as in No. 14, 3rd class.

Omit the words "in the last practice in 9" on page 47.

Page 48; lines 6 to 8 now read "These will be entered singly with their results in the rough musketry practice sheets, in the company musketry book, and in the return of ammunition."

Line 22, after " class " add " If only one of these classes is represented, both prizes are given to it."

Line 29; omit " both in the cases of under-officers and men."

Lines 32 and 33; for "completed the practices for which conditions are prescribed " read "fulfilled the conditions."

Lines 34 and 35; for "practices for which conditions are prescribed" read " principal practices."

9th and 10th lines from bottom; for "man's breadths" read " bullseyes."

Page 49, line 8; omit from " with the proviso " to end of sentence.

Line 20; omit "of the line regiment bearing the same number."

Line 22; omit "under § 2, 6, of the Landwehr-Ordnung."

Page 49. The following paragraph is inserted between § 31 and § 32:—

Prizes of Honour for exceptionally good Shooting.

Prize shooting for officers, and also for under-officers, takes place annually, and, according to the results of the firing, prizes are given in the name of His Majesty to the best shots among the officers, and to the best shots among the under-officers.

The prizes for officers are swords, those for under-officers are watches.

The sword, of the usual pattern, will have a suitable inscription, and the name of the officer to whom it is granted, engraved on the hilt; similarly the name of the under-officer, and the occasion of bestowal, will be engraved on each watch.

In future each Army Corps will receive two prizes yearly—one for the best shot among the Infantry officers, and one for the best shot among the Infantry under-officers. To the XIth Army Corps four instead of two prizes will be given in the even-number years, two for the best and second best shots among the Infantry officers, and two for the best and second best shots among the Infantry under-officers. In future, too, two prizes will annually be placed at the disposal of the Inspection of Infantry Schools—one for the best shot among the officers, and one for the best shot among the under-officers of the Under-Officers' Schools (Preparatory Schools).

The shooting is to be held on the ranges in the months of July or August. Within the period stipulated the firing days are to be so fixed by the troops concerned, that the firing may take place under the most favourable extraneous conditions.

All captains and lieutenants of the corps concerned who are present in the garrison on the day fixed for the firing, and have to go through the target practice with the troops, are bound to take part in the prize shooting, the only exceptions being those who are prevented owing to unavoidable duty, sickness, &c. The staff officers of the Army Corps are entitled to take part.

For the under-officers' prizes, all those under-officers compete who have to go through the target practices, are present in garrison on the day fixed for the shooting, and are not prevented by unavoidable duty, sickness, &c.

Officers and under-officers on command at stations where prize firing is held take part in the firing there, if they have not already competed with their own troops in the same year.

Officers and under-officers who have once received a sword or watch for exceptional shooting are excluded from further competition.

Target: ring target, with 24 rings; radius of ring 24, ·98 inch, the radii of the other rings increasing by ·98 inch each. The rifle and ammunition supplied by the Army Corps.

Distance, 150 metres (164 yards); number of shots, 7, viz., 3 standing with rest, 4 standing with hands free. Before commencing the firing, a trial shot (which must be declared such in advance) is allowed.

The decision depends first and foremost on the total of the rings hit. If this be equal, the decision is given by the last shot, or if necessary the last but one, or last but two, &c.

Infantry regiments report the name of the best shot among their officers and under-officers, together with their scores, to Army Corps head-quarters; under-officers' schools, to the Inspector. (In the XIth Army Corps, in even-number years, the names of the best and second best shots among the officers and under-officers are reported.)

By the 5th September every year the Army Corps authorities, in accordance with these reports, communicate the name of the best shot among the officers and the best among the under-officers (including schools) of the Army Corps, together with their scores, to the General War Department, length of sword scabbards for the officers being required. (In the XIth Army Corps the second best shot among the officers and under-officers is communicated every second year.)

The General War Departments in accordance with the communications above mentioned, transmits the prizes directly to the corps, and the latter arrange for their being presented to the respective recipients with suitable ceremony.

The names of the officers and under-officers distinguished by the bestowal of these prizes are to be made known within the Army Corps (Infantry Schools) and to be reported to His Majesty when the musketry returns are submitted.

Page 49, bottom of page; add "If circumstances permit of the company commander instituting similar exercises with the under-officers, it will be advantageous in many respects."

Page 50, line 8; for "them" read "the rules laid down in the Infantry Drill Regulations as regards training for combat."

Lines 10 to 17; omit from "For the officers" to "difficult."

Line 18; omit "half Züge."

13th and 14th lines from bottom; omit "as well as firing by half Züge of war strength."

11th line from bottom; omit "of war strength."

10th line from bottom; instead of "companies on the same footing" read "larger detachments."

9th line from bottom; omit "half."

8th line from bottom; for "Züge and companies" read "larger detachments."

Page 51, line 6; after "only" add "garrison drill grounds being made use of so far as they are suited for the purpose, or in artillery practice grounds."

Line 13; omit "500 or" and "550 to."

Page 51, line 24; after "markers" add "and workmen."

Line 27; add "The routine between the firing detachment and the markers must be thoroughly regulated and practised beforehand."

Paragraph 35 now reads:—"If the rifle is properly used, a hit may be expected with each shot, as follows:

Within 250 metres (273·4 yards) against all objects;

Up to 350 metres (382·7 yards) against a single man kneeling;

Up to 500 metres (546·8 yards) against a file kneeling (the men close together);

Up to 600 metres (656·1 yards) against a file standing (the men close together) or a single horseman.

The regulations for target practice give the necessary indications as to the employment of sights and the selection of points of aim."

Page 52. The whole of § 36 is cancelled and the following substituted:—

"The fighting training of the man as laid down in the Infantry Regulations (training as a rifleman) constitutes at the same time the preparation for individual firing."

Page 53. The first sub-paragraph of § 37 now reads as follows:—"The exercises, which ought to develop the self-reliance of the man and his power of deciding for himself in individual combat, are carried out against figure targets and their several modifications, and against targets representing horsemen. Interesting problems of a simple nature in the domain of field service, or of musketry combat in the absence of any fire direction, will form the basis of the exercises."

Line 29; omit "and interest awakened."

Line 31; omit sentence "The magazine, &c."

Line 36; the sub-paragraph beginning "Each man," is altered as follows:—

"Each man either fires from the same spot at several objects which appear in succession at different distances, or he changes his position by advancing or retiring. The possibility of observing the effect of fire must he taken advantage of, and another man must accompany the firer, taking up a position, near him, observing the effect of his shot and communicating it to him. In this way the habit of observing the effect of fire, which is so important and only to be acquired by much practice, is impressed upon the men "

"The man judges the distance, decides whether he will fire and (after his estimate of the distance has been corrected, if necessary, by the instructor) states what sight he will use, and the point he will aim it; he then presents, aims and fires. It must be observed that in order to strengthen the man's confidence in his skill as a marksman, and in his weapon, the shot should be fired, as a rule, only at a distance within the limits at which a hit is probable, and on this point the firer must be instructed. In carrying out the exercises alluded to at the beginning of this paragraph, the decision of the firer, as to whether he ought to fire at the objects which appear, must be made to depend solely upon the nature of the exercise or the actual phase of the combat. If the firer has already acquired considerable skill, the instructor allows him to act independently on the appearance of the object, and does not discuss his several proceedings until the shot has been fired."

Page 54, line 6. The sub-paragraph now reads as follows :— "The importance of the exercises forbids that all the cartridges reserved for individual firing should be expended by the man on one day. The men of the youngest class will proceed to practise individual firing as soon as they have received sufficient training in firing; officers, under-officers, and old soldiers will commence the exercises as soon as possible after the beginning of the new musketry year."

Line 20; for "400" read "600."

2nd to 7th line from bottom; omit.

Page 55, line 6; for "800 metres" read "1,000 metres (1,093 yards)."

Lines 8 to 14; for "400 metres" read "600 metres (656·1 yards)" and for "800 metres" read "1,000 metres."

Page 56, lines 3 and 5; for "600 metres" read "800 metres (875 yards)."

Lines 9 to 11; omit.

Lines 17 to 22 now read "Men aim at the bottom of the object. If any other point of aim is considered more favourable, it will be ordered by the officer, &c., directing the firing; if no one is directing the firing, it will be selected by the firer himself."

Line 26. This paragraph now commences "With regard to the direction of fire, and fire discipline, reference must be made to the Infantry Regulations." The remainder of the paragraph to line 16 on page 63 is transferred to those regulations, with the exception of lines 14 to 31 on page 58, which alone are retained in this paragraph.

Page 63, lines 19 to 21; omit from "The magazine."

Lines 37 and 38; for "half Züge, Züge, and companies made up to war strength," read "Züge or in stronger bodies."

Line 38; omit remainder of paragraph (to line 3 page 64) and substitute "The first object of the exercises is to make all ranks of the firing detachment conversant with fire discipline, and to train the leaders in their duties during the varying phases of the fight. Nevertheless, in the arrangement of the exercises, it must be borne in mind that situations ought to be reproduced which will require the men to act independently."

Page 64, lines 9 to 15; omit from "The appearance."

Line 21; for "necessary for criticising the operations," read "or when the exercise is concluded."

Last line; omit to end of line 6, page 65.

Page 65, lines 7 to 15; omit and substitute "In the case of men of the youngest annual class these exercises are to be conducted in connection with individual firing; in the case of other men, at all periods of the year."

5th and 6th lines from bottom; omit.

Page 66. The first sub-paragraph now reads "A good shot, sitting behind a table with rifles on the rest, fires 9 shots at a ring target at 350 metres with the small flap; one rifle being an accurate shooter, one shooting too high, and the third too short. Point of aim, middle of the bullseye."

Line 8; for "5" read "9."

Lines 16 and 17; distances are now 250, 350, 500 and 600 metres.

Lines 18 to 21 now read "Good shots, sitting behind a table with rifles on the rest, each fire 25 shots at the distances above mentioned, with corresponding sights, at a ring target or a white target of the same size with clearly visible and correspondingly placed (centre) mark. Rifles to be accurate shooters; point of aim, the centre of the bullseye or mark."

Line 30; for "400" read "450 and 500."

Lines 34 to 42 now read,

"With the standing sight and with the small flap at distances of 50, 100, 150, 200 and 250 metres;

With the small flap only at 300 and 350 metres;

With the 450 and 500-metre sight at 100, 200, 300, 400 and 450 metres.

With the 500-metre sight only at 500 metres.

Point of aim; bottom of the target or mark at its lower edge. Ring target, or a white target of the same size."

Page 67, lines 13 to 19; sub-paragraph 4 is omitted.

Page 68, lines 9 to 13; omit. The letter-press (not the figures) of Appendix B and Appendix C (pages 97 to 100) are introduced here, before sub-paragraph 2, with certain alterations which will be noted in their proper place.

Line 15; omit "of greater or less strength."

Lines 18 and 19; omit and substitute "shown in figures on pages 98, 99."

Line 21; omit "as they lie on the rests."

Lines 32 to 38; omit.

Page 69; § 46 is re-written, as follows :—

The exercises will be published yearly by the War Ministry in the month of July, in the "Armee-Verordnungs-Blatt."

The firing must be concluded within ten days of the receipt of the number of the "Verordnungs-Blatt" containing the order. This period may be extended in special cases for individual battalions by the superior authorities of the arm. Report to accompany the Musketry Reports (page 80).

Preliminary practices with ball cartridge are forbidden.

In the case of isolated battalions, the exercise will be conducted by the battalion commander. If several battalions are quartered together in the same garrison, the regimental commander directs the exercises, but may from time to time depute the field officer of the regimental staff to perform the duty for him.

It is not necessary that the companies of a corps should shoot on the same day; but if a company has begun the exercise, the latter must be concluded on the same day, even if bad weather sets in.

Before the firing commences, the directing officer satisfies himself as to the correctness of the target measurements. Officers are charged with the supervision of the markers and the recording of the results. The hits are to be given in whole numbers. In calculating the percentages, fractions of $\frac{1}{2}$ and over are to be reckoned as 1, fractions under $\frac{1}{2}$ are not counted.

Order of dress; as for the principal practices in target practice. The weighting of the knapsack is effected at the range.

The report to be made on the individual musketry inspection is attached to the musketry reports and signed by the officer who conducts it. At the end of the report a statement as to the weather, temperature, light and wind, is to be added.

Page 70. The form of report is omitted (to middle of page 71).

Page 71, lines 3 to 6 from bottom; omit and substitute "The same is done if any cartridges destined for an exercise in the open field are not entirely shot off."

Page 72, lines 26 and 29; for "preliminary" read "preparatory."

Page 76, line 17; omit "total."

Page 77, line 21 from bottom; omit "Instead of the exercises shown above."

Line 20 from bottom; for "ones" read "exercises."

Lines 16 and 17 from bottom; omit sentence "The expenditure, &c."

Page 78, line 14; add "(ring target, firing at the band)."

Line 18; omit (M=hit &c.)

Line 19; for "man's breadth" read "the band or bullseye."

Lines 21 and 22; omit "A number crossed through denotes outside the man's breadth."

Line 23; omit.

Line 24; omit "target" and "man's breadth and."

Line 11 from bottom; should be " | ·+ +. ·10 | "

Line 9 from bottom; should be "+· 9 ·9 6. 3· "

Page 79, line 19; add " with statement whether the rifle shoots accurately, too high or short."

Lines 25 to 29; omit from " with aiming &c.," and substitute "statement as to probability of hitting of single shot, § 35."

Lines 12 and 13 from bottom; omit " and Return of ammunition " and " and 4."

Lines 8 to 11 from bottom now read, " The battalions prepare a musketry report on Form 5 [now numbered 4] and forward it to the regiment together with the company returns."

Line 7 from bottom; omit " and returns of ammunition."

Page 80, line 1; omit " the Emperor and King."

Page 82. The following alterations are made in the Musketry sheet.

Practice No. 1. Ring target, 2 bands, 3 bullseyes.
    ,,   No. 2. Ring target, 3 bullseyes.
    ,,   No. 3. Ring target, 26 rings, 2 shots within 9.
    ,,   No. 5. 3 figures.
    ,,   No. 8. 4 hits.
    ,,   No. 9. 5 hits, 35 rings, 3 shots within 8.
    ,,   No. 10. Figure target, 4 figures, in 30 seconds.

In last line but one of Remarks; omit " complete."

Page 83. In sub-paragraph 2 omit " to complete the strength of the company."

Page 84. Musketry report, 3rd and 4th lines from bottom; omit " for which conditions are prescribed."

Pages 86 and 87. Form 4, " Return of ammunition," is omitted.

Page 89. At the foot of Form 5 [now Form 4], insert note to remarks (column 9):—" In the case of exercises held at the ranges it is sufficient to note the month, while for exercises in the open field the day and place must be entered."

Page 90, line 11; add " or fix a higher or lower one."

Line 19; for " the rings must not pinch " read " the barrel must neither be pinched nor fit loosely in the muzzle ring."

Lines 20 to 26; alter as follows:—" The ring target will be used, a rectangle 15·7 inches high by 3·9 inches broad being marked out by perpendicular pencil lines drawn 1·96 inches to the right and left of the central line of the target, and joined by two horizontal lines at the height of the outer boundary of ring 8 above and ring 10 below."

Line 32; for " lower cross patch " read " bullseye."

Line 34; omit from " described " to end of sentence.

4th line from bottom, omit " at the band."

Page 91, lines 32 to 34; prefix " for the revolver only " and transfer to the end of sub-paragraph 2 (after " gases ").

Page 92, line 17; after " cartridges " insert " (in 20 full packets)."

Lines 21 and 22 ; omit, and substitute "100 shots are fired from each rifle (contents of 20 packets), and 40 shots from each revolver, and the result of each shot noted."

Line 24, omit " chamber of the."

Lines 29, 30, 31 ; omit "and the number of ring-shaped marks stamped on the surface showing the number of times they have been used again."

8th line from bottom ; for " 250 rifle cartridges " read " 150 rifle cartridges (contents of 30 packets)."

Page 93, line 2 ; for " 23·6 " read " 31·4."

Line 8 ; for "comparative" read " trial."

Line 11 ; for " 50 " read " 30."

Line 19 ; for " 50 " read " 30 "; for " 25 " read " 15."

Line 21 : for " 25th and 26th " read " 15th and 16th."

Line 22 ; for " 25 " read " 15."

Line 23 ; for " 25th and 26th " read " 15th and 16th."

Line 26 ; for " 7·8 " read " 5·9."

Figure 15 is replaced by the following :—

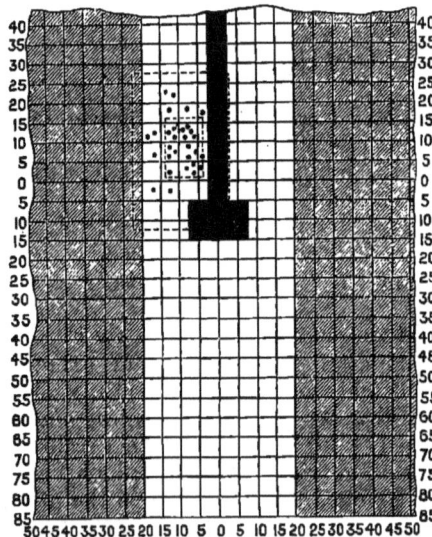

Page 94, line 1; for " 5·9," " 23·6 " and " 15·7 " read " 3·9," " 15·7 " and " 9·8 " respectively.

Line 26; for " in man's breadth " read " in middle third of target."

Figure 16 is unaltered, with the exception that the ground of the target is entirely white and no man's breadths shown.

Page 95, lines 6 and 7; for " on a man's breadth " read " in the middle third of the target."

Line 12 ; insert the following :—

" Testing ammunition in which the casing strips from the

bullet. (In these bullets the metallic casing becomes separated from the bullet before impact and splits. They are recognised by a peculiar sound and cause misses). If more than 1·5 per cent. of the ammunition shows this fault at the target practices, the troops concerned must at once forward 1,000 cartridges of the same lot to the Rifle Testing Committee.

Any rifle, in the firing of which this fault of the cartridge is continually happening, must also be sent to the above-named committee, even if less than 1·5 per cent. of the ammunition on the whole shows the defect in question."

Page 96. The whole of Appendix A is transferred to § 9, page 17.

Page 97, 2nd line from bottom; add " Rifle slings long."

The figures in Appendix B are transferred to § 9, page 17; the letter-press is transferred to page 68, with the following alterations:—

Page 99, lines 11 and 12; omit, and add " The knob of the bolt lies against the right side of the rear picket."

The last seven lines on this page and the first six on page 100 are altered as follows:—

" The firer draws the rifle backward only for the purpose of charging it with a new packet, after which the rifle must be accurately replaced in its proper position. In loading from the magazine, the rifle is to be retained fixed in its position. The firer must stand upright as may be required, otherwise proper fire effect will be jeopardized.

In firing with the rifle M/71. 84 the same mode of proceeding is to be adopted. When pickets are used, the rifle must be placed so far forward that the knob of the bolt shall touch the rear picket."

Page 100, line 9; after " rest " insert " or pickets."

Figure 1 in Appendix C is transferred to § 9, page 17; the description of the steel mantlet is transferred to page 68, with the addition after " soil " (line 20), " A second plate is fixed as close as possible behind the first." The figures and description of shelter trench loopholes are erased altogether.

Figure 3, in plate at end, is altered as follows:—

The distances on ground line marked 765 yards, 774 yards, &c., are now increased (from left to right) to 874·9 yards, 889·2 yards, 903·6 yards, 918·1 yards, 932·5 yards, and 947 yards.